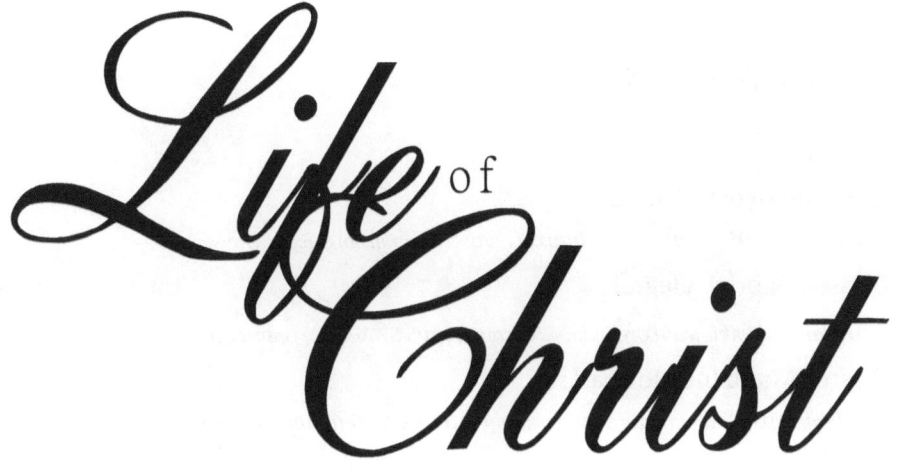

MARIA VALTORTA'S
Life of Christ

Treasured by

Saint Teresa of Calcutta,

Blessed María Inés Teresa Arias,

and Blessed Gabriel Allegra

© Regina Angelorum Press, LLC, 2019.

© Regina Angelorum Press, LCC, 2019

All rights reserved. In accordance with the U.S. Copyright Act of 1976, no part of this publication may be reproduced, distributed, or transmitted in any form or by any means, including photocopying, recording, or other electronic or mechanical methods, without the prior written permission of the publisher, except in the case of brief quotations embodied in critical reviews and certain other noncommercial uses permitted by copyright law.

Cover design by Raya Cotton

Cover photos:

Saint Teresa of Calcutta:

Manfredo Ferrari [CC BY-SA 4.0 (https://creativecommons.org/licenses/by-sa/4.0)]

Blessed Gabriel Allegra:

https://upload.wikimedia.org/wikipedia/commons/5/57/Allegra_Gabriele.jpg

Blessed Maria Ínes Teresa Arias:

Tstude at the German language Wikipedia [CC BY-SA 3.0 (https://creativecommons.org/licenses/by-sa/3.0)]

All cover photos belong to their rightful owners and are licensed under Creative Commons. Owners do not endorse this publication in any way.

ISBN: 978-0-9861151-2-7

REGINA ✦ ANGELORUM ✦ PRESS

Dedicated

to

The Poor Souls in Purgatory

May All Who Read This Pause to Pray:

May the souls of the faithful departed,

through the mercy of God

rest in peace.

TABLE OF CONTENTS

Preface 1

1. Saint Teresa of Calcutta 3

2. Blessed María Inés Teresa Arias 11

3. Blessed Gabriel Allegra 15

4. Response to Some Objections 31

5. Blessed Allegra's Critique of the *Poem* 59

Appendix I: Discover the Fruits of the *Poem* Yourself 76

Appendix II: Documents Regarding Testimony
of St. Teresa of Calcutta and Blessed María Inés 85

About the Authors 88

Preface

Father Anthony Pillari's thesis and now his publishing, with Stephen Austin, of this new book, *Maria Valtorta's Life of Christ*, fills me with great joy. I am grateful not only for the high quality of this academic work with its profound level of research, but also for how it contributes to a deeper understanding of God's gifts in troubled times like ours.

In early spring 1972, when I had just announced that I was going to the United Kingdom for further studies, an aunt of mine told me she wanted to give me a gift for my time abroad. I immediately hoped for some financial support and was quite disappointed when she instead handed me a box with ten books: the ten volumes of Maria Valtorta's *Poem*. As it turned out, these books were much more precious than money because they changed my life and laid the foundation for my vocation to the priesthood.

The prayerful daily reading of Maria Valtorta's great work was a catechetical formation for a young man like me who was advancing in academic studies but who was ignorant in matters pertaining to his faith. The daily reading of the Bible and the daily prayerful reading of the *Poem* turned out to be a "student's retreat" and a great gift from God. May these gifts multiply a hundredfold.

With my best wishes and God's blessing,

Msgr. Leo Maasburg
National Director of the Pontifical Mission Societies in Austria and a close associate of Mother Teresa of Calcutta

1

SAINT TERESA OF CALCUTTA

At times, over the course of several years, I observed Mother Teresa traveling with three books: the Bible, her breviary, and a third book. When I asked her about the third book she replied that it was the *Poem of the Man-God* by Maria Valtorta. When I further asked about its contents, Mother Teresa replied, "Read it." The book was one of the five English volumes of "The Poem of the Man-God."[1]

As Mother Teresa's confessor, Fr. Maasburg traveled and worked closely with her for years.[2] In addition to the Bible and her breviary, what was this third book that Mother Teresa chose to carry with her? It is a life of Christ written by a laywoman in the 1940s and first published in 1956, a life of Christ that readers—among whom St. Teresa of Calcutta, Blessed María Inés Teresa Arias, and Blessed Gabriel Allegra—have found so enriching that it has since been translated into more than twenty languages and has sold hundreds of thousands of copies.[3] Who was the author of this work? Some famous writer? No. Rather, it was an unknown, bed-ridden, Italian woman.

---

[1] L. Maasburg, Testimony regarding Blessed Teresa of Calcutta's use of the writings of Maria Valtorta, given in writing to Fr. Anthony Pillari, April 25, 2016. Commenting on this in a June 7, 2018 e-mail interview with Fr. Pillari, Msgr. Maasburg wrote, "I was curious as to what Saint Mother Teresa would read besides the Bible. I was delighted to hear that it was my beloved *Poem* which by then I had read to the last letter. When the Saint said, "Read it," I felt confirmed in my decision to have read it (many were opposed and the Index was still too close). But I didn't feel the immediate urge to show off with my knowledge of a book Mother Teresa was reading... Her example (reading the *Poem*) sparked my desire to read it again and again. Still today on my trips I carry with me ten, fifteen chapters of the *Poem*—my copies have fallen apart long ago—and I read it with a feeling of coming home."

[2] Msgr. Maasburg is the author of *Mother Teresa of Calcutta: A Personal Portrait*, San Francisco, CA: Ignatius Press, 2015.

[3] As of December 31, 2016, 367,000 complete editions (containing all 10 volumes) of The *Poem of the Man-God* have been sold by the primary publisher in England. However, this figure does not include editions of the work published in nine other languages and so the total figure is likely approaching 500,000. (From L. Venditti, January 3, 2017, via e-mail).

Maria Valtorta

Maria Valtorta was born in Caserta, Italy, on March 14, 1897, into a middle-class family. In her youth, she had the fortune of receiving a classical education before moving to Viareggio, Italy, in 1924, where she spent most of her remaining life. Maria Valtorta was a member of the Third Order Servites of Mary. She was well-educated, industrious, intelligent, and gifted.

In 1920, at the age of 23, while walking down the street with her mother, she was struck in the back with an iron bar by an anarchist delinquent. She was confined to a bed for three months and then recovered enough to be able to move around again. In 1925, she read the autobiography of St. Thérèse of the Child Jesus, and, inspired by it, offered herself as a victim soul to the Divine Merciful Love. Five years later, she took private vows of virginity, poverty, and obedience, and then (after much deliberation and preparation) offered herself also as a victim to Divine Justice.

God accepted her offer. As a result of complications from her injury in 1920, as well as having contracted numerous terrible illnesses that caused her great pain, she was bedridden beginning in 1934 and was forced to remain bedridden for the remaining 28 years of her life. She suffered greatly.

Her confessor, Fr. Migliorini, was struck by her virtue and commanded her to write her autobiography. Less than a month after the conclusion of her autobiography, on Good Friday, she heard a supernatural voice instructing her to write and dictating to her. Fr. Migliorini commanded her to write down everything.

Over the next four years (1943–1947), she would write more than 13,200 pages of "dictation" (what she believed to be supernatural visions and messages) while sitting up in bed. The majority of these pages would form the life of Christ entitled in English *The Poem of the Man-God,* or later *The Gospel as Revealed to Me* (hereafter the work will simply be referred to as "the *Poem*"). Having died on October 12, 1961, her body was later transferred to the Capitular Chapel in the Grand Cloister of the Basilica of the Most Holy Annunciation in Florence.[4] Fr. Gabriel Roschini, O.S.M., world-renowned Mariologist, presided over the relocation of the remains of Maria Valtorta from Viareggio to the Grand Cloister of the Basilica of the Most Holy Annunciation, including presiding over the Mass, giving the appropriate discourse for this occasion, and giving the blessing for her burial.[5] The inscription on her tomb reads: *"Divinarum Rerum Scriptrix"* (Writer of Divine Things).

Publication of the *Poem*

On February 26, 1948, Pope Pius XII received in audience three priests of the Order of Friar Servants of Mary (Servites): Fr. Romualdo Migliorini, Valtorta's spiritual director; Father Corrado Berti, professor of dogmatic and sacramental theology at the Marianum Pontifical Faculty of Theology in Rome; and Fr. Andrea Cecchin, Prior of St. Alexis Falconieri College in Rome.[6] Pius XII had been given a typewritten copy of Valtorta's still unpublished work some months earlier, and these three

---

[4] E. Pisani, *Pro e Contro Maria Valtorta,* 5th Edition, Isola del Liri (FR), Italia: Centro Editoriale Valtortiano, 2008. See also M. Miravalle, "Response to Various Questions Regarding 'The Poem of the Man-God,'" in *Mother of All Peoples* (online journal), April 15, 2006. http://www.valtorta.org.au/Valtorta-Miravalle.html (1 April 2016).

[5] See also G. Roschini, *The Virgin Mary in the Writings of Maria Valtorta,* Kolbe Publications Inc., 1989. Page XIII in the Publisher's Notice. ISBN-13: 9788879870863. For more details, see http://www.valtorta.org.au/Father-Gabriel-Roschini-Valtorta.html

[6] Notice of audience with Pius XII, in *Osservatore Romano (OR),* February 27, 1948, 48. Fr. Cecchin was also professor of liturgy, patristics, and patrology at the Marianum. The process for his beatification is currently underway.

priests would report that Pius XII told them at the audience: "Publish this work as it is. There is no need to give an opinion about its origin, whether it be extraordinary or not. Who reads it, will understand."[7] However, in 1949, officials of the Holy Office summoned Fr. Berti to appear before them. They commanded him to turn over all manuscripts. Fr. Berti testified that he was not permitted to speak and was thus unable to reveal to the Holy Office the command given him by Pope Pius XII to publish her work.[8]

In 1952, ten scholars, among whom was Archbishop Alfonso Carinci, Secretary of the Sacred Congregation of Rites, petitioned Pius XII to permit the work to be published.[9] Nonetheless, there was no forthcoming papal intervention. As related in Fr. Berti's testimony, convinced that Pope Pius XII's words from the 1948 audience, "Publish the work as it is," had precedence in the matter, Fr. Berti still sought to publish the *Poem*, and it was published for the first time in 1956.[10]

On December 16, 1959, under John XXIII, the Holy Office placed the first edition of the work on the Index.[11] The decree was published in the January 6, 1960, edition of *L'Osservatore*

---

[7] M. Miravalle, "Response," no. 1. See also E. Pisani, *Pro e contro*, 63.

[8] C. Berti, A Testimony on Maria Valtorta's *Poem of the Man-God*, December 8, 1978, Signed in Rome. Available at http://www.bardstown.com/~brchrys/Corberti.html.

[9] See E. Pisani, *Pro e contro*, 65–94. Msgr. Carinci was Secretary to the Congregation of Sacred Rites from 1930–1960 and charged with discerning between authentic saints and frauds. Having visited Valtorta multiple times, he had a favorable opinion of her and her writings. See also the correspondence between Msgr. Carinci and Valtorta in Valtorta, *Lettere a Mons. Carinci*, Isola del Liri, (FR) Italia: Centro Editoriale Valtortiano, 2006.

[10] We will not here enter into a discussion of whether or not Fr. Berti's actions were appropriate. Just a few years later, as will be seen in chapter 4, the Index was abolished and the publication of the *Poem* became henceforth licit. Hence, we simply note here the explanation that Fr. Berti himself gave for his actions.

[11] Congregation for the Doctrine of the Faith (CDF), Decree placing *Il Poema di Gesù* and *Il Poema dell'Uomo-Dio* on the Index, 16, December 1959, in AAS, 52 (1960), 60.

Romano, along with an anonymous article which asserted that the work had been placed on the Index because the publisher had violated canon 1385 (*CIC*/17) which required any writings treating of religious matters to receive the imprimatur prior to publication.[12] The Index would be abrogated just a few years later, and interest in Valtorta's writings would increase significantly in the following decades.

Of Saints and Blesseds

In the Apostolic Constitution *Divinus perfectionis magister*, the Church explains the reasons for proposing some of the faithful who were "outstanding in the practice of Christian virtues" for the "pious devotion of, and imitation by, the faithful."[13] In other words, the Church explains why she beatifies and canonizes people. Proposing someone for the pious devotion of the faithful means proposing him or her as a heavenly intercessor. Three significant steps occur in the later stages of the process of canonization: the promulgation of a decree on the heroic virtues of the Servant of God, the act of beatification, and the act of canonization. As Msgr. Robert Sarno of the Congregation for the Causes of Saints asserts, "only beatification gives the confirmation of the intercessory power of the Servant of God."[14] Once a Servant of God has been beatified, the faithful can have full confidence in the Blessed's intercessory power and imitability.

---

[12] "Una vita di Gesù malamente romanzata," *OR*, January 6, 1960, 4.

[13] John Paul II, Apostolic Constitution on the Revised Procedure in Causes of Saints *Divinus perfectionis magister*, January 25, 1983, in *Acta Apostolicae Sedis (AAS)*, 75, I (1983), 349–355, English translation in W. Woestman, *Canonization: Theology, History, Process*, 2nd ed., Ottawa: Faculty of Canon Law, Saint Paul University, 2014, 214.

[14] R. Sarno, e-mail reply to Fr. Anthony Pillari, August 16, 2016.

With regard to imitability, the Church proclaims that "when we consider the life of those who have faithfully followed Christ [...] we are most safely taught the path by which [...] we can arrive at that perfect union with Christ, which is holiness."[15] This does not mean that the individual was infallible, but that the Church invites the faithful to have particular confidence and trust in imitating the lives of those who have been declared blessed or canonized, assuring us that we are "most safely" taught the path by which we can arrive at holiness when we imitate them. Monsignor Sarno specifies that the Church gives us the assurance that those declared blessed or who are canonized led a "totally heroically virtuous life," meaning that they practiced the four cardinal virtues and the three theological virtues to a heroic degree. The Congregation looks closely at the last five to ten years of the individual's life to "verify the reaching of a heroic practice of all the Christian virtues."[16] This point will be important when considering the testimonies of Blessed María Inés Teresa Arias and Blessed Gabriel Allegra.

But what does *Divinus perfectionis magister* mean with regard to the example of Mother Teresa, cited above? In virtue of the Church's canonization of Mother Teresa, we know that in imitating her we are "most safely taught the path" by which we can arrive at holiness, since she possessed the virtues to a heroic degree. This does not mean that she was infallible, but it does mean that her example is a relevant one when discerning the value of a Life of Christ such as the *Poem*, particularly when considered in conjunction with the following examples.

---

[15] John Paul II, *Divinus perfectionis magister*, in Woestman, *Canonization*, 215.
[16] R. Sarno, e-mail reply, August 16, 2016.

2

BLESSED MARÍA INÉS TERESA ARIAS

Blessed Mother Maria Inés Teresa of the Most Blessed Sacrament (1904–1981) is famous for founding the Congregation of Claretian Missionaries in 1945, which has grown to include 36 missionary houses in 14 countries. Cardinal Amato described her as "generous in work, fervent in prayer, humble, self-sacrificing and always ready to help."[17] She took final vows in 1933 and lived a cloistered religious life until 1949. In 1945 she received authorization from Rome to found a new contemplative-active religious congregation.

On April 21, 2012, María Inés Teresa Arias was beatified. Also the foundress of the Poor Clare Missionary Sisters of the Blessed Sacrament, she wrote in 1978, "I am very attached to the reading of the work *The Poem of the Man-God*. Truly it has become one of the most beautiful sources of spiritual reading."[18] In addition to using the work for her own spiritual reading, Arias promoted it to others. As Sister Urlanga testified, "Our Reverend Mother liked [the *Poem*] very much and asked me to order the series of four volumes in Spanish and Italian for the thirty-five houses that she had founded up until then, and that were scattered all over the world. She also gave them as gifts to Bishops, Priests, and other persons."[19]

---

[17] Zenit News Staff, "Mother Maria Inés Teresa Beatified in Mexico City," April 23, 2012. Available at https://zenit.org/articles/mother-maria-ines-teresa-beatified-in-mexico-city.

[18] "Io sono molto affezionata alla lettura dell'opera 'Il Poema dell'Uomo Dio.' Veramente è diventata una delle fonti di lettura spiritual più bella." M. I. T. Arias, letter expressing gratitude for writings of Valtorta, May 22, 1978, in *ibid.*, 46.

[19] "…yo por encargo de N. Rev. Madre hice todos los pedidos para surtir a las 35 casas esparcidas por el mundo que hasta entonces habia fundado Nuestra Madre porque a ella le gustaba mucho y aparte regaló a Obispos, Sacerdotes y personas la serie de los 4 tomos en español e italiano." M.G. Uranga L., private letter, July 19, 2001, in A. Pillari, "The Current Juridic and Moral Value of the Index of Forbidden Books," 47. Available at https://ruor.uottawa.ca/bitstream/10393/37164/4/Anthony%20PILLARI.pdf.

These actions were taken during the last five to ten years of Blessed María Inés' life,[20] the period of a blessed's life that the Congregation for Saints scrutinizes carefully to ensure that the individual practiced heroic virtue. Thus, we have the assurance that Blessed María Inés was exercising virtue to a heroic degree, including the virtue of prudence, during the time that she took these actions of promoting the *Poem* to her sisters throughout the world, as well as to bishops, priests, and others. While this does not render her actions infallible, the Church declares that in imitating her, particularly during this last period of her life, we are "most safely taught the path" by which we can arrive at holiness.

---

[20] The 1978 letter was written just three years before her death. Since the first Spanish volume did not appear until 1976, Arias' actions to obtain the work for the 35 houses she had founded and others must have taken place during the last five years of her life.

3

BLESSED GABRIEL ALLEGRA

On September 12, 2012, Gabriel Allegra (1907–1976) was beatified. Blessed Gabriel Allegra was born in Catania. He was a learned and world-renowned exegete, a theologian, and a missionary priest in the Order of the Friars Minor, which he entered at the age of 16. After being ordained in 1930, he departed to China and distinguished himself as an exemplary missionary and man of culture. As a St. Jerome of our time, he was the first to translate the entire Bible into Chinese, and his work had the support and acknowledgement of successive popes from Pius XI to Paul VI. He founded the Studium Biblicum Franciscanum in Beijing in 1945 for this work. Those who knew Blessed Gabriel commented on his humility and complete dedication to souls.

The only twentieth century Scriptural exegete to be beatified, he discovered Valtorta's writings in 1965 and studied them intensely.[21] Father Leonard Anastasius, vice-postulator of the Friars Minor, spoke of the contributions that Blessed Gabriel gave to the analysis of Maria Valtorta in two letters to the editor:

"I am an assiduous reader of the Work of Maria Valtorta. In these days there have come under my eyes some handwritten pages found in the notebooks of Father Gabriel Allegra's diary, which speak of the previously mentioned writer [Valtorta]. You know that Father Allegra was a great admirer and diffuser of Maria Valtorta's writings, so much so that he may be called a 'Valtortian.' I have the joy of communicating to you that last January 14th, at Hong Kong, the process for his beatification

---

[21] To facilitate the work of readers who desire prompt access to quotes from Blessed Gabriel on particular topics, a few of his quotes have been repeated at different points in this book. The same practice has been followed with a few other parts of the analysis. The hope of the authors is that this repetition will permit the book's use as a quick reference on various subjects.

was opened. I am its Vice-Postulator; and having found among his writings some pages which concern Maria Valtorta, I have made photocopies of them to send them off to you. They will be very useful to you. The judgment of Father Allegra is very valid, since he had been a biblical scholar of world renown" (Letter of February 3, 1984).

"I have learned with pleasure the news given me, that is, that in the next number of the *Bollettino Valtortiano* [*Valtorta Bulletin*] you will speak of our Father Allegra whose cause for beatification has already been introduced. Truly, he can be considered a 'Valtortian.' He was very enthusiastic about the 'Poem of the Man-God.' He spoke of it frequently in his various encounters. In letters from him which I am reading, I often find his exhortations to read the 'Poem.' It had been he who advised me to read it in 1970. And from then on until today I have never stopped reading it. This very day I have sent to you some other photocopied pages of the writings of Father Allegra in which he speaks in a marvelous way of Maria Valtorta" (Letter of April 12, 1984).[22]

After several years of study and prayer, Blessed Gabriel Allegra wrote:

"After the Gospels, I do not know another life of Jesus that can compare to the *Poem*, as I do not know any other lives of St. Peter and St. John which make the characters of these two Apostles so alive.... In treating the mystery of Mary's Compassion, it seems to me that Valtorta, through her breadth, profundity and psychological probing of the Heart of the Virgin,

---

[22] The original Italian can be found in *Bollettino Valtortiano*, no. 29, January–June 1984, 114–116, 03036 Isola del Liri (FR), Italia: Edizioni Pisani / Centro Editoriale Valtortiano srl. Viale Piscicelli, 89/91. English translation by Br. Chrys Castel, OCSO.

surpasses even St. Bonaventure and St. Bernard. Could she have done this without having supernaturally seen and heard?"[23]

Much impressed with the *Poem*, he urged others to read it, and he continued to study it during the last ten years of his life. He held, while respecting an eventual judgment of the Church, that the work came from the Spirit of Christ, and that "It is a work that makes one grow in the knowledge of the Lord Jesus and of His Holy Mother."[24] Such assertions are significant because they were made by one whom the Church assures us not only possessed to a heroic degree the virtues of prudence and faith, but who also had as his life's work the study of Sacred Scripture, who was an expert in this domain, and who analyzed the *Poem* at the peak of his scholarly knowledge.[25] By the Church's proclamation through his beatification that when we imitate him we "most safely" follow the path that leads to holiness, we can follow his prudential judgment with confidence.

Two centuries earlier, in 1816, the Church beatified another scholar, Alphonsus Liguori. A few years after his beatification, but before his canonization, and well before he was proclaimed a Doctor of the Church, the Sacred Penitentiary clarified that "one could safely follow the teaching of St. Alphonsus, without even seeking other opinions,"[26] though this did not mean

---

[23] "Dopo i Vangeli, io non conosco un'altra vita di Gesù che si possa paragonare al Poema, come non conosco altre vite di San Pietro o San Giovanni che rendano così vivi i caratteri dei due Santi Apostoli.... Nel trattare il mistero della Compassione di Maria, pare a me che la Valtorta, per ampiezza, profondità e scandaglio psicologico del Cuore della Vergine, superi perfino San Bonaventura e San Bernardino. Poteva farlo senza aver supernaturalmente visto e sentito?" In Pisani, *Pro e contro*, 129–130.

[24] *ibid.*, 143. See also *ibid.*, 121.

[25] Allegra would continue to work actively as a scholar up until the time of his death in 1976. His analysis of the *Poem* began in 1965, when he could approach the text with the benefit of forty years' experience as a Scriptural exegete.

[26] A. Cummings, *The Servant and the Ladder*, Leominster, England: Gracewing, 2014, 131.

that Alphonsus was infallible nor that other opinions were false. While that judgment was a singular one concerning St. Alphonsus, it sheds light on the Church's assertion that "when we consider the life of those who have faithfully followed Christ [...] we are most safely taught the path by which [...] we can arrive at that perfect union with Christ, which is holiness," and how it can be received with regard to the theological writings of a beatified scholar.

Given Blessed Gabriel Allegra's unique combination of expertise as a world-renowned scriptural exegete, his heroic practice of the virtues, and an intense study of the *Poem* during the last 11 years of his life when he was at the peak of his scholarly knowledge, sections of his analysis of the *Poem* are quoted below at some length. His comments are grouped according to categories to assist those seeking to find the Blessed's thoughts on one topic or another.

Divine Inspiration

"I hold that the Work [of Valtorta] demands a supernatural origin. I think that it is the product of one or more charisma and that it should be studied in the light of the doctrine of charisma, while also making use of the contributions of recent studies of psychology and related sciences which certainly could not have been known by old theologians like Torquemada, Lanspergius, Scaramelli, etc.

"[...] Now, without anticipating the judgment of the Church which to this moment I accept with absolute submission, I allow myself to affirm that since the principal criterion for the discernment of spirits is the Word of the Lord: *From their fruits you will know them...*, (*Mt 7:16*), and with the good fruits which the *Poem* is producing in an ever growing number of readers, I think that it comes from the Spirit of Jesus."[27]

"[…] In the Church there is the Spirit, and hence, there are the charisma of the Spirit. I myself think that only through a charism of the Holy Spirit, solely with His help, could a poor sick woman of limited biblical culture write, in the space of three years, 15,000 pages which when printed are the equivalent of ten volumes. And what pages! I note also that certain of the Lord's Discourses of which the principal subjects are only hinted at in the Gospels, are developed in this Work with a naturalness, with a connection of thought so logical, so spontaneous, so coherent with the time, the place, the circumstances, as I have not found in the most famous exegetes.

"[…] No one could make me believe that a poor, sick woman has written the *Poem* solely in virtue of her fervent religious feeling—all the more so since she did not see the various pictures or scenes from the life of the Lord in chronological order but rather, contrary to such order, scattered or confusingly re-presented to her throughout the space of three years.

"[…] Having well determined the nature of the charism of the Spirit and the reality of His action in Maria Valtorta, what attitude ought the Christian to assume in reading these admirable evangelical pages?

"It seems to me that the same practical conclusion imposes itself for whoever has read and studied the documents of the History of the Apparitions of Paray le Monial, Lourdes, Fatima, Syracuse….

---

[27] Extract taken from Blessed Gabriel Allegra's critique of Maria Valtorta's work written in June 1970 during a hospital stay in Macao. The original Italian can be found in E. Pisani, *Pro e contro Maria Valtorta* (6th Edition), Isola del Liri (FR), Italia: Centro Editoriale Valtortiano, 2017, 139–148. ISBN-13: 9788879872959.

"And with the same degree of faith, and in the measure which the Lord Jesus and the Church desire it, I believe in it.

"[...] In two long chapters, Valtorta describes what she saw and heard during the night of Good Friday, the day of the Sabbath, and the night of the Sabbath [Holy Saturday]. The little that I have read on the Sorrowful Mother on this subject remains in generalities; it cannot be compared to these powerful and very tender pages of Maria Valtorta. I cannot for anything convince myself that they are a simple meditation of a pious woman. No. This soul has seen and heard! The Finger of God is here!

"[...] For a book so engaging and challenging, so charismatic, so extraordinary even from just a human point of view as is Maria Valtorta's *Poem of the Man-God*—for such a book I find the theological justification in the *First Epistle to the Corinthians 14:6*, where St. Paul writes: 'If I come to you, brethren, speaking in tongues, how shall I benefit you unless I bring you some revelation or knowledge or prophecy or doctrine?'"

"In this Work I find so many revelations which are not contrary to, but instead complete, the Gospel narrative. I find knowledge: and such knowledge in the theological (especially Mariological), exegetical, and mystical fields, that if it is not infused I do not know how a poor, sick woman could acquire and master it, even if she was endowed with a signal intelligence. I find in her the charism of prophecy in the proper sense of a voice through which Valtorta exhorts, encourages and consoles in the name of God and, at rare times, elucidates the predictions of the Lord. I find in her doctrine: and doctrine such as is sure; it embraces almost all fields of revelation. Hence, it is multiple, immediate, luminous.

"[...] The figure, the virtues, the mission of the Madonna have been and are described by many of the holy, wise and devoted; and yet no one does it with the simplicity of Maria Valtorta in her *Poem of the Man-God*.

"Valtorta has seen and heard; the others, for the most part, have only thought and meditated. But what surprises me the more is the sure vision of the gifts of Mary most holy.

"[...] *The Poem*, when completed, makes us better understand the Gospel, but it does not contradict it. I still do not know how to explain to myself, and perhaps I will never know, how the Lord had ever shown His earthly life to a soul of the 20th Century, but I believe in the Love which can do all. And I think also that this Omnipotent Love never asked such a sacrifice of a poor, sick woman for herself alone, but asked it for all the faithful, at least for those who believe in the charisma diffused in His Church by the Spirit, the Head of Christ.

"[...] Finally, I observe that the Work of Valtorta is indirectly a proof of the historicity of the Gospels: they are, yes, a catechism, a *kerigma* [proclamation], but based upon the *martyria* [testimony] of witnesses chosen and approved by God. Quite different than *Formgeschichte* [*Form Criticism*]!

"The effectiveness of the Word of God is conditioned by the quality of the terrain in which it falls. Man has the dreadful gift of liberty through which he can say 'No' even to God!

"Keeping in mind the parable of the sower, the liberty of man, and my own persuasion that the *Poem of the Man-God* is the Work of Jesus first and of Maria Valtorta next, the reaction of readers before this Work is expressed thus:

"The Work of the *Poem* meets: distracted readers, honest readers, pious readers, critical and hypocritical readers....

"The theologian and exegete should be at the same time among both the honest and the critical readers.

"[...] This double series of Discourses is completed by the Conversations of Jesus with the Apostles, by His polemics in the Temple and at Jerusalem or on the roads of Palestine, and finally, by His gracious, Heavenly confidences with the Apostles, the men and women Disciples, and especially with His Most Holy Mother.... What a work, this *Poem*! No, it is not a poor human work. There is in it the Finger of God.

"[...] In the *Poem of the Man-God*, Mammon is often equivalent to Satan; it is another name for Satan. Now I find that even Theodore Zahn, in his commentary on the *Gospel of St. Matthew* has, for philological reasons, arrived at the same conclusion.

"*The Poem* reserves for us many such surprises—which confirms the fact that we have before us, not the reveries of a sick woman, but rather the affidavit of a witness: only a witness, certainly, but one so worthy of faith.

"[...] After the Gospels, I do not know of another life of Jesus which can be compared with the *Poem*, just as I do not know any other lives of St. Peter or St. John which make the characters of the two holy Apostles so living. I cite these two because there is something about them in the Scriptures, while of the other Apostles we have almost only the names. Now, all the characters are always so well delineated and so consistent with themselves, that we find ourselves before a dilemma: either the Writer is a genius of Shakespearean or Manzonian stamp, or she has actually seen.

"I opt for—rather I am compelled to choose—the second horn of the dilemma."[28]

---

[28] These passages were written by Blessed Gabriel in the late 1960s. The original Italian can be found in *Bollettino Valtortiano*, no. 29, January–June 1984, 114–116, 03036 Isola del Liri (FR), Italia: Edizioni Pisani / Centro Editoriale Valtortiano srl. Viale Piscicelli, 89/91. English translation by Br. Chrys Castel, OCSO.

"Since I have read and re-read the *Poem of the Man-God* of Maria Valtorta, I have no taste any more for biblical-gospel novels. [...] But since I am convinced that M. Valtorta 'has seen' in a way that I have still not succeeded in explaining completely to myself, while Witbuley, like Lloyd Douglas, and others...have only rethought, as more or less great artists, the pages of the Gospel, I am not allowed to be so demanding. No one asks of apocryphal writings what only the Gospels can give us."[29]

"I would like for a single instant to find myself in Rome to take you by your ears and pull them very, very hard, as when the bells once used to be loosed on Holy Saturday morning! But do you know that the *Poem of Jesus* [sic] has detached me from my studies of Holy Scripture? And it makes me weep and laugh with joy and love. But I will not go on! I do not believe that genius could thus complete the Gospel narration: the Finger of God is here! Quite different from *Formgeschichtemethode*! [*Form Criticism Method*] I sense in this book the Gospel, or better, the intoxicating perfume of the Gospel. [...] This book is for me an act of Divine Mercy for the Church, for simple souls, for hearts which are evangelically children."[30]

"Valtorta Never Falls into Theological Error"

"And what makes me marvel the more is that Valtorta never falls into theological error; on the contrary, she renders the

---

[29] Letter, June 18, 1970. The original Italian can be found in *Bollettino Valtortiano*, no. 30, July–December 1984, 118, 03036 Isola del Liri (FR), Italia: Edizioni Pisani / Centro Editoriale Valtortiano srl. Viale Piscicelli, 89/91. English translation by Br. Chrys Castel, OCSO.

[30] Letter to Fr. Fortunato Margiotti in Rome, July 30, 1965. The original Italian can be found in *Bollettino Valtortiano*, no. 31, January–June 1985, 122, 03036 Isola del Liri (FR), Italia: Edizioni Pisani / Centro Editoriale Valtortiano srl. Viale Piscicelli, 89/91. English translation by Br. Chrys Castel, OCSO.

mysteries revealed more easy for the reader, transposing them into a popular and modern language.

"[…] The Mercy of the Lord in the *Poem* is never separated from the demands of the Divine Justice, as also all the revelations—which He makes—not only do not contradict the Gospel, but harmonize perfectly with the economy of the Faith in which those saved should live, and which constitutes the framework of the whole Bible and especially of the New Testament."[31]

Good Fruits

"Now, without anticipating the judgment of the Church which to this moment I accept with absolute submission, I allow myself to affirm that since the principal criterion for the discernment of spirits is the Word of the Lord: *From their fruits you will know them…*, (Mt 7:16), and with the good fruits which the *Poem* is producing in an ever growing number of readers, I think that it comes from the Spirit of Jesus."[32]

"Concerning Valtorta's exegesis, there would be enough to write a book. Here I limit myself to reaffirming that I find no other works of eminent scripture scholars which, like Valtorta's *Poem*, complete and clarify the Canonical Gospels so naturally, so spontaneously, with such liveliness. In these latter there is continual talk of crowds, of miracles, and we have some outlines of the Discourses of the Lord. In the *Poem of the Man-God*,

---

[31] These passages were written by Blessed Gabriel in the late 1960s. The original Italian can be found in *Bollettino Valtortiano*, no. 29, January–June 1984, 114–116, 03036 Isola del Liri (FR), Italia: Edizioni Pisani / Centro Editoriale Valtortiano srl. Viale Piscicelli, 89/91. English translation by Br. Chrys Castel, OCSO.

[32] Extract taken from Blessed Gabriel Allegra's critique of Maria Valtorta's work written in June 1970 during a hospital stay in Macao. The original Italian can be found in E. Pisani, *Pro e contro Maria Valtorta* (6th Edition), Isola del Liri (FR), Italia: Centro Editoriale Valtortiano, 2017, 139–148, ISBN-13: 9788879872959.

however, the crowds move, shout, are agitated; the miracles, you would say, are seen; the Discourses of the Lord, even the most difficult in their conciseness, become of solar clarity.

"[...] There is no pseudo-religiosity in the works of St. Gertrude, St. Teresa, in the *Meditations on the Life of Christ* of Fr. John of Calvoli, in *The Mystical City of God* of Ven. Mary of Agreda, in the writings of St. Charles of Sezze.... And likewise, I do not find it either in the *Poem*. Rather, I find in it a living and complete exposition of almost all Catholic doctrine and morality. But what makes me love it more is that the *Poem* itself pushes the reader to read the Bible with love and humility, and to listen with love and humility to the teaching of Holy Mother Church."[33]

"I am pleased to see the *Poem of the Man-God* translated into other tongues, because I am certain that through reading it many will grow in the knowledge and love of the Lord Jesus. I entrust this desire of mine to St. Clare and to M. Lucia Mangano."[34]

"If Holy Mother Church should have to disavow this book because it is a question of private revelations, no one will be more glad to obey than I. But if, as I think, the Church will allow it to circulate through the hands of the faithful, like the revelations of Anne Catherine Emmerich or Ven. Mary of Agreda, I think that it will do an immense good."[35]

---

[33] These passages were written by Blessed Gabriel in the late 1960s. The original Italian can be found in *Bollettino Valtortiano*, no. 29, January–June 1984, 114–116, 03036 Isola del Liri (FR), Italia: Edizioni Pisani / Centro Editoriale Valtortiano srl. Viale Piscicelli, 89/91. English translation by Br. Chrys Castel, OCSO.

[34] Letter, January 8, 1970. The original Italian can be found in *Bollettino Valtortiano*, no. 30, July–December 1984, 118, 03036 Isola del Liri (FR), Italia: Edizioni Pisani / Centro Editoriale Valtortiano srl. Viale Piscicelli, 89/91. English translation by Br. Chrys Castel, OCSO.

[35] Letter to Blessed Gabriel's uncle Joachim, Vicar in San Giovanni La Punta

"...I end, dear Mario, by recommending to you the reading of the voluminous but fascinating *Poem of the Man-God* of Maria Valtorta: Fr. Margiotti has procured it for me and Fr. Pieraccini bought it for the Library. I assure you that this work brings one near the Lord and stimulates us strongly to meditate on the Gospel: I would like to say so many other things about it, but I do not want to with paper and ink, at least for now. I embrace you fraternally."[36]

"It is a Work that makes one grow in the knowledge and love of the Lord Jesus and His Holy Mother."[37]

On Maria Valtorta

"The Writer confesses repeatedly that she is only a 'mouthpiece,' a 'phonograph,' one who writes what she sees and hears, while remaining 'crucified on a bed.' Hence, according to her, the *Poem* is not her own, it does not belong to her, it was revealed, shown to her. She does nothing else but describe what she has seen, report what she has heard, while also participating with all her heart of a woman and a devoted Christian in the visions. From this intimate participation of hers is born the antipathy she feels for Judas and, on the contrary, the intense affection she feels for John, for the Magdalene, for

---

(Catania), August 5, 1965. The original Italian can be found in *Bollettino Valtortiano*, no. 31, January–June 1985, 122, 03036 Isola del Liri (FR), Italia: Edizioni Pisani / Centro Editoriale Valtortiano srl. Viale Piscicelli, 89/91. English translation by Br. Chrys Castel, OCSO.

[36] Letter to Fr. Mario Crocco, Vicar in Castellammare di Stabia (Napoli), August 29, 1965. The original Italian can be found in *Bollettino Valtortiano*, no. 31, January–June 1985, 122, 03036 Isola del Liri (FR), Italia: Edizioni Pisani / Centro Editoriale Valtortiano srl. Viale Piscicelli, 89/91. English translation by Br. Chrys Castel, OCSO.

[37] Letter to Blessed Gabriel's cousin Leonie Morabito, Poor Clare Sister in Caltanissetta, from Jerusalem, Monday of Holy Week, 1974. The original Italian can be found in *Bollettino Valtortiano*, no. 31, January–June 1985, 122, 03036 Isola del Liri (FR), Italia: Edizioni Pisani / Centro Editoriale Valtortiano srl. Viale Piscicelli, 89/91. English translation by Br. Chrys Castel, OCSO.

Syntyche..., and I do not even speak of the Lord Jesus and of the most holy Madonna towards whom at times she pours out her heart and her love with words of passionate lyricism worthy of the greatest mystics of the Church."[38]

On Maria Valtorta's Autobiography

"The *Autobiography* of Maria Valtorta departs from other similar works, even if written by saints. It is powerful and original to the point of making me think often of that of B. Cellini from its style: robust, lively and spontaneous.

"It is moreover a dramatic book, because the drama stands out in the nature of things and facts: the drama is born, I would say, from the character of Valtorta's mother who, unfortunately, had little or nothing of the heart of a wife or mother. The description, so lively, of this egotistical woman weighs on the reader and makes him read with pain these pages of her daughter, of that daughter who becomes the 'voice' of Jesus and who writes *The Poem of the Man-God*. What a difference of character between mother and daughter! And what sort of heroism, and how much, in Maria. What a trial, what crosses, what martyrdom of the heart!

"The Valtorta family is completely opposite to that of St. Francis. In the latter, the father, Peter of Bernardone, does not understand his son, who instead was always understood by his mother, the gracious madonna Pica. In the Valtorta family, however, the father loves and understands his daughter, whom her mother does not understand at all and makes her always suffer.

---

[38] Extract taken from Blessed Gabriel Allegra's critique of Maria Valtorta's work written in June 1970 during a hospital stay in Macao. The original Italian can be found in E. Pisani, *Pro e contro Maria Valtorta* (6th Edition), Isola del Liri (FR), Italia: Centro Editoriale Valtortiano, 2017, 139–148, ISBN-13: 9788879872959.

"The heart of this woman is still more gloomy than that of the Prince father of the nun of Monza, and one is left so grieved by it in reading these pages because they have been written—naturally in obedience—always by her daughter.

"The style is vigorous and very lively, copious and so colorful that it perhaps surpasses that of the *Poem of the Man-God* itself. These are pages rich with thought and psychological soundings which help us to understand the spiritual physiognomy of the mouthpiece of Jesus: Maria Valtorta."[39]

"...And now I thank you for the *Autobiography* of Maria Valtorta, which absolutely occupies a place apart among all the autobiographies of men and women saints which I have read; like that of B. Cellini, it stands out among all other similar works of our literature.

"It is painful to read what it says of her mother, and yet it seems to me that it was this intimate, continuous, torturing martyrdom which prepared Maria Valtorta for the sublime gifts of the visions and contemplations which she later received; in sum, it was this that had prepared her to be the mouthpiece of the Lord Jesus.

"The language seems to me more varied and vigorous than that of the *Poem of the Man-God*, which also is so fresh and lively.

"[...] I hope that the editors continue to publish all the works of this soul, virile in her humility, a soul which often makes one think of St. Catherine of Siena."[40]

---

[39] These passages were written by Blessed Gabriel in the late 1960s. The original Italian can be found in *Bollettino Valtortiano*, no. 29, January–June 1984, 114–116, 03036 Isola del Liri (FR), Italia: Edizioni Pisani / Centro Editoriale Valtortiano srl. Viale Piscicelli, 89/91. English translation by Br. Chrys Castel, OCSO.

[40] Letter to Fr. Fortunato Margiotti in Rome, May 24, 1969. The original Italian can be found in *Bollettino Valtortiano*, no. 31, January–June 1985, 122, 03036 Isola del Liri (FR), Italia: Edizioni Pisani / Centro Editoriale Valtortiano srl. Viale Piscicelli, 89/91. English translation by Br. Chrys Castel, OCSO.

4

RESPONSE TO SOME OBJECTIONS

The combined testimony of Saint Teresa of Calcutta, Blessed María Inés Teresa Arias, and Blessed Gabriel Allegra should render any prospective reader confident—one would think eager!—to read the *Poem*. If the only beatified scriptural exegete of the twentieth century highly praises a life of Christ, declaring that "After the Gospels, I do not know of another life of Jesus which can be compared with the *Poem*..."[41] "...I find no other works of eminent scripture scholars which, like Valtorta's *Poem*, complete and clarify the Canonical Gospels so naturally, so spontaneously, with such liveliness. [...] What makes me marvel the more is that Valtorta never falls into theological error..."[42] "...I find in it a living and complete exposition of almost all Catholic doctrine and morality. But what makes me love it more is that the *Poem* itself pushes the reader to read the Bible with love and humility, and to listen with love and humility to the teaching of Holy Mother Church..."[43] Who would not be eager to read such a book?

Yet, most Catholics are unaware of the testimony of Blessed Allegra, as well as that of Blessed María Inés and St. Teresa of Calcutta. In addition, some are confused by the fact that the *Poem* was placed on the Index. Even though the Index was abolished in 1966, some are unsure as to whether or not this still reflects negatively on the *Poem*. For the benefit of those with such questions, a canonical analysis of the question of the Index's enduring juridic and moral value is presented here. For those without such questions, please feel free to skip this chapter.

---

[41] These passages were written by Blessed Gabriel in the late 1960s. The original Italian can be found in *Bollettino Valtortiano*, no. 29, January–June 1984, 114–116, 03036 Isola del Liri (FR), Italia: Edizioni Pisani / Centro Editoriale Valtortiano srl. Viale Piscicelli, 89/91. English translation by Br. Chrys Castel, OCSO.

[42] *ibid.*

[43] *ibid.*

The following is an excerpt—chapters 2 and 3—from "The Current Juridic and Moral Value of the Index of Forbidden Books":[44]

2 – Abrogation of the Index and Its Subsequent Juridical and Moral Status

On December 7, 1965, Paul VI renamed and restructured the Holy Office as the "Congregation for the Doctrine of the Faith" (CDF) through his motu proprio *Integrae servandae*.[45] As would become apparent in some of the dicastery's first official acts—its notification of June 14, 1966,[46] and decree of November 15, 1966[47]—positive ecclesiastical law regarding the Index had been abrogated.

2.1 – Abrogation of the Index

Paul VI asserted that the Church "employs different instruments according to the various times and human cultures" and that, "because there is *no fear* in love (1 Jn 4:18), the defense of the faith is now better served by promoting doctrine."[48] Thus, *Integrae servandae* signaled a significant

---

[44] "The Current Juridic and Moral Value of the Index of Forbidden Books," by Fr. Anthony Pillari was a successful J.C.L. thesis at the University of St. Paul that received an A+ by the faculty. An electronic version of the full thesis can be obtained at the following link: http://www.valtorta.org.au/JCL-Thesis-on-the-Index-and-Valtorta.pdf.

[45] Paul VI, Motu Proprio *Integrae servandae*, December 7, 1965, in *AAS*, 57 (1965), 952–955. English translation of the norms in *Canon Law Digest (CLD)*, vol. 6, 358–359; complete translation with Introduction at www.vatican.va. [= Paul VI, *Integrae servandae*].

[46] Congregation for the Doctrine of the Faith, Notification regarding the abolition of the Index of Forbidden Books, June 14, 1966, in *AAS*, 58 (1966), 445, English translation in *CLD*, vol. 6, 814–815 (= CDF Notification).

[47] Congregation for the Doctrine of the Faith, Decree regarding canons 1399 and 2318 no longer in force, November 15, 1966, in *AAS*, 58 (1966), 1186, English translation in *CLD*, vol. 6, 817–818 (= CDF Decree).

[48] Paul VI, *Integrae servandae*, Introduction.

shift in the Church's manner of exercising its duty of vigilance with regard to teachings that could be harmful to the Gospel message. However, the full implications of the motu proprio with regard to the Index were not immediately clear.

Six months after the promulgation of *Integrae servandae*, the Congregation issued a notification regarding the abolition of the Index of Forbidden Books. It proclaimed that "the Index remains morally binding, in light of the demands of natural law, insofar as it admonishes the conscience of Christians to be on guard for those writings that can endanger faith and morals. But, at the same time, it no longer has the force of ecclesiastical law with the attached censure."[49] Nonetheless, requests for clarification continued to be sent to the CDF. So, five months after its notification on the matter, the Congregation issued a decree to clarify that canons 1399 and 2318 (*CIC*/17) were abrogated. This meant that books on the Index were no longer prohibited in virtue of positive ecclesiastical law, and anyone who had incurred censures by publishing, reading, retaining, selling, translating into another language, or in any other way communicating prohibited works to others was to consider the censure remitted.

It would be difficult to overstate the significance of this change. Whereas the above-mentioned actions had been considered mortal sins in virtue of their violation of positive ecclesiastical law, they were now not sins at all, because the positive ecclesiastical law no longer existed. Such actions *might* be sins due to the violation of the natural law, but the primary arbiter in this matter was now the "conscience of Christians."[50]

---

[49] CDF Notification, in *CLD*, vol. 6, 814.
[50] *ibid.*

2.2 – Current Juridic Status

What is the current juridic status of the Index of forbidden books? As the Congregation's notification regarding the abolition of the Index of books stated, the "Sacred Congregation for the Doctrine of the Faith, after having asked the Holy Father, announces that the Index [...] no longer has the force of ecclesiastical law with the attached censure."[51] Since the Index no longer has any force in ecclesiastical law, it no longer has juridic status.[52] Hence, with regard to all the works that Catholics had been forbidden to read because they were on the Index, Catholics were free to read them.

It may be helpful to consider an example. A Catholic who in 1964 was aware that John Stuart Mill's *Principles of Political Economy* had been placed on the Index of Forbidden books and who nonetheless chose to read the work, without any special permission from ecclesiastical authorities, was considered to have committed a mortal sin.[53] The individual was considered to have committed a grave sin of disobedience because he had violated the prohibition in positive ecclesiastical law against reading works placed on the Index, not because the book's content was gravely sinful. The latter might be the case for some works on the Index, in virtue of the natural law, but that is a separate question that will be examined below. However, if a Catholic in 1967, fully aware that Mill's work had been placed on the Index, still chose to read it, he would not be guilty of any sin by virtue of the fact that the work was on the Index. Yet,

---

[51] *ibid.*

[52] Compare with the continuing prohibition in ecclesiastical law of membership in the Masons, as analyzed in E. Condon, "The Enduring Force of the Canonical Prohibition of Masonic Membership in the 1983 Code of Canon Law," in *The Jurist*, 74 (2014), 289–352.

[53] Jone, *Moral Theology*, 274. See also Betten, *The Roman Index*, 43.

there would remain the question of whether it was sinful to read the work based on its content.

2.3 – Moral Value

The notification declares that the "Index remains morally binding, in light of the demands of the natural law, insofar as it admonishes the conscience of Christians to be on guard for those writings that can endanger faith and morals."[54] Thus, the notification echoes the fundamental principle that, even where one had permission to read books, this freedom "in no way exempts one from the prohibition of the natural law against reading books that present a proximate spiritual danger to oneself."[55]

Everyone has an obligation by virtue of the natural law to avoid writings that would harm his faith or morals. Prior to the abrogation of the Index, each Catholic who received special permission to read works that had been placed on the Index had to decide, according to his conscience, if a given work would present a proximate spiritual danger to his soul. After the abrogation of the Index, every Catholic now finds himself in this position. Hence, each Catholic must now make a prudential judgment, according to his conscience, whether reading a work that had been on the Index would present a proximate spiritual danger to him.

The Church teaches that "moral conscience, present at the heart of the person, enjoins him at the appropriate moment to do good and to avoid evil."[56] The Church describes

---

[54] CDF Notification, in *CLD*, vol. 6, 814.

[55] *CIC*/17, c. 1405 §1.

[56] *Catechismus Ecclesiae Catholicae*, Libreria editrice Vaticana, 1997, English translation *Catechism of the Catholic Church*, 2nd ed., New York: Doubleday, 2003, no. 1777.

this judgment of conscience as involving 1) perceiving the "principles of morality," 2) applying those principles to the circumstances one is faced with, via a "practical discernment of reasons and goods," and 3) making a concrete judgment about acts to be performed.[57] Hence, when faced with a decision as to whether to read a particular book—regardless of whether the book had been on the Index—the judgment of conscience incorporates these three elements. If one judges, according to one's conscience, that a book would present a proximate spiritual danger to one's soul, and one still decides to read the book, one commits a sin. However, if one judges that a book would not present a proximate spiritual danger, then there is no sin committed in reading it, even if it had been on the Index.

In evaluating a work that had been on the Index, it is good to recall that works were placed there for a variety of reasons. Some works were placed there because they had been published without prior Church approval, not because of harmful content.[58] Other works were on the Index for disciplinary reasons rather than because of heretical or obscene content. At times, a book was on the Index because ecclesiastical authorities determined that it might be dangerous for some persons to read at that particular point in history. Years later, when such dangers were judged no longer to be present, the book was removed from the Index.[59]

The current moral value of the Index is that it can provide information that should be weighed as one discerns whether to read a work. It would be erroneous to consider the Index morally binding in such a way that it would be a sin to read any

---

[57] *ibid.*, no. 1778.
[58] See Bettencourt, *The Imprimatur*, 53. See also Wolf, *Storia dell'Indice*, 25–28.
[59] Betten, *The Roman Index*, 18.

work ever placed on it. On the contrary, the Church asks each Catholic to make a prudential judgment as to whether a given work would be a proximate spiritual danger to him.

Was a given work placed on the Index because it lacked ecclesiastical approval prior to its publication rather than because of its content? Or, on the contrary, was it on the Index because its content was judged heretical or obscene? Was its content such that it was considered dangerous for some persons at that point in history to read but where such danger no longer exists today? Such considerations must be weighed in conscience, also recognizing that, without any opportunity for updating the Index these past fifty years, some of it is likely to be obsolete.

2.4 – Censorship in the 1983 Code

Positive ecclesiastical law concerning the publication and use of books would undergo a significant change with the promulgation of the 1983 Code of Canon Law. The change was so significant that just one year after the Code's promulgation, James Coriden would pen an article entitled "The End of the Imprimatur." As Coriden explains:

"From the sweepingly broad categories of 'whatever pertains to religious or moral disciplines' and 'anything of special religious or moral interest' [*CIC*/17 c. 1385 §§ 1 and 2] [the imprimatur] was reduced to biblical and liturgical texts, prayer books, catechisms, school textbooks dealing with religious or moral matters, and religious literature sold or given away in churches. The range of writings requiring the imprimatur was narrowed down to those few basic categories of works which are considered most 'official' and whose need for accuracy calls for special screening. All other theological and religious writings are exempted from the requirement."[60]

Previously, the imprimatur had been required for any book that touched upon the areas of religion or morality, and it was forbidden to read any such book published without the imprimatur.[61] After the promulgation of the 1983 Code, writings that always require an imprimatur for publication are editions of Sacred Scripture, liturgical books, books of prayers, collections of ecclesiastical decrees and acts, and catechisms.[62] Books whose content pertains to Sacred Scripture, theology, canon law, ecclesiastical history, or religious or moral disciplines do not normally require an imprimatur, except when they are to be used as "texts on which instruction is based in elementary, middle, or higher schools."[63] Furthermore, while the code reaffirmed the duty and right of bishops to condemn writings which could cause harm to faith or morals, the indicated condemnation is something vastly different from what had taken place when condemned works were placed on the Index. The manner of condemnation most often used in the Church since the abrogation of the Index can be best understood by looking at the Congregation for the Doctrine of the Faith's actions in this regard.

2.5 – Censorship by the Congregation for the Doctrine of the Faith

Paul VI signaled the change in the Church's manner of exercising its role of vigilance in *Integrae servandae*. In

---

[60] J. Coriden, "The End of the Imprimatur," in *The Jurist*, 44 (1984), 340.
[61] See *CIC*/17 c. 1399 §1 and c. 1385.
[62] See *CIC*/83 cc. 825-828.
[63] *CIC*/83 c. 827 §2.

renaming and restructuring the Holy Office, he proclaimed, "because there is no fear in love (1 Jn 4:18), the defense of the faith is now better served by promoting doctrine, in such a way that...those who err are gently called back to the truth."[64] The CDF asserted that the Church "trusts in the mature conscience of the faithful."[65] In implementing this approach, the CDF has chosen to make use primarily of notifications of errors in works. These notifications are meant to alert members of the Church to the errors or dangers in these works, but they do not impose any juridic prohibitions or censures, thus leaving Catholics, in most cases, free to make use of them.[66] For example, after an extensive examination of the works of Fr. Jon Sobrino, the Congregation found his writings to contain errors in key doctrines, such as the divinity of Jesus Christ, the Incarnation of the Son of God, and the salvific value of his death.[67] Nonetheless, rather than imposing any sort of censure on the author or prohibition with regard to the publication or reading of the works in question, or with regard to their use as textbooks, the Congregation limited itself to asserting that "it was decided to publish this *Notification*, in order to offer the faithful a secure criterion, founded upon the doctrine of the Church, by which to judge the affirmations contained in these books or in other publications of the author."[68] Even in cases

---

[64] Paul VI, Integrae servandae, Introduction.

[65] CDF Notification, CLD, vol. 6, 814.

[66] See, for example, CDF, Notification on the works of Fr. Jon Sobrino, S.J., November 26, 2006, in *AAS*, 99 (2007), 181–194 [= CDF, Notification Sobrino]; Notification regarding certain writings of Fr. Marciano Vidal, C.Ss.R., February 22, 2001, in *AAS*, 93 (2001), 545–555; Notification concerning the writings of Fr. Anthony De Mello, S.J., June 24, 1998, in *AAS*, 90 (1998), 833–834; and Note on the book *The Sexual Creators, An Ethical Proposal for Concerned Christians* by R. André Guindon, O.M.I., January 31, 1992. English translations on the CDF website of www.vatican.va.

[67] CDF, Notification Sobrino, no. 1.

[68] *ibid.*

such as this, the Congregation normally takes the approach of limiting its condemnation to the publication of a notification pointing out the errors in question. The Congregation entrusts to each individual the discernment and judgment as to whether to read, publish, or make use of such texts.

A recent case, in which the Congregation took stronger measures, involves Margaret Farley's book *Just Love. A Framework for Christian Sexual Ethics*. In addition to pointing out the errors in this work, the Congregation declares:

"With this Notification, the Congregation for the Doctrine of the Faith expresses profound regret that a member of an Institute of Consecrated Life, Sr. Margaret A. Farley, R.S.M., affirms positions that are in direct contradiction with Catholic teaching in the field of sexual morality. The Congregation warns the faithful that her book *Just Love. A Framework for Christian Sexual Ethics* is not in conformity with the teaching of the Church. Consequently it cannot be used as a valid expression of Catholic teaching, either in counseling and formation, or in ecumenical and interreligious dialogue."[69]

On rare occasions, the Congregation applies censures to the author.[70] For example, after examining Roger Haight's book, *Jesus Symbol of God*, the Congregation determined that the work contained serious doctrinal errors which were causing "grave harm to the faithful."[71] These errors involved fundamental doctrines such as the pre-existence of the Word, the divinity of

---

[69] CDF, Notification regarding the book *Just Love. A Framework for Christian Sexual Ethics* by Sr. Margaret A. Farley, R.S.M., March 30, 2012, in *AAS*, 104 (2012), 505–511.

[70] In some cases, this includes even the excommunication of the author. See, for example, the Notification concerning the text "Mary and Human Liberation" of Fr. Tissa Balasuriya, O.M.I., January 2, 1997, in *Origins*, 26 (1996), 528–530.

[71] CDF, Notification regarding the book "Jesus Symbol of God" of Fr. Roger Haight, S.J., December 13, 2004, in *AAS*, 97 (2005), 194–203, Introduction.

Jesus, the Holy Trinity, the salvific value of the death of Jesus, his resurrection, and the salvific mediation of Jesus and of the Church. The Congregation judged these errors to be "serious doctrinal errors contrary to the divine and Catholic faith of the Church. As a consequence, until such time as his positions are corrected to be in complete conformity with the doctrine of the Church, the Author may not teach Catholic theology."[72] Nonetheless, the Congregation did not impose any prohibition on the use of this work for personal study or as a textbook (at least at the university level). Rather, it left each individual to discern whether or not to read, publish, or in any other way make use of the text.

In some cases, the Congregation has gone beyond alerting the faithful to errors in a work or applying a censure to the author. For example, after examining the works of Vassula Ryden, the Congregation requested the intervention of bishops so that "no opportunity may be provided in their Dioceses for the dissemination of her ideas." It also invited the faithful "not to regard Mrs. Vassula Ryden's writings and speeches as supernatural."[73]

3 – Case Study: Maria Valtorta

Although the Index was abrogated more than fifty years ago, debates about its current moral and juridical value continue to this day.[74] We will now examine a particular text that, despite having been placed on the Index, has been published in more than twenty languages and sold hundreds of thousands of

---

[72] *ibid.*, Conclusion.

[73] CDF, Notification on the writings and activities of Mrs. Vassula Ryden, October 6, 1995, in *AAS*, 88 (1996), 956–957.

[74] See, for example, M. Pacwa, "Is the Poem." See also M. Miravalle, "Response."

copies.[75] This is a life of Christ written by Maria Valtorta in the 1940s and placed on the Index on December 16, 1959.[76]

As previously noted, and to reinforce the cogent portions of the above text, the following is provided: Valtorta was born into a middle-class family in Caserta, Italy, on March 14, 1897. At the age of twenty-three, she was randomly, violently attacked and struck in the back by a young man. As a consequence, her health began to decline. By the age of thirty-seven, she was permanently confined to bed. Nine years later, still bedridden, she began to record in handwritten notebooks what she believed to be mystical experiences of the lives of Jesus and Mary. Between 1943 and 1947, she would write almost 13,200 pages of "dictation" of what she believed to be supernatural visions and messages. The majority of these pages would come to form the life of Christ entitled in English *The Poem of the Man-God* (= "the *Poem*"), or later *The Gospel as Revealed to Me*. A few years after her death on October 12, 1961, her body was transferred to the capitular chapel in the Grand Cloister of the Basilica of the Most Holy Annunciation in Florence.[77]

3.1 – Valtorta's Work Placed on the Index

On February 26, 1948, Pius XII received in audience three priests of the Order of Friar Servants of Mary (Servites): Fr. Romualdo Migliorini, Valtorta's spiritual director; Father

---

[75] As of December 31, 2016, 367,000 complete editions (containing all ten volumes) of the *Poem of the Man-God* have been sold by the primary publisher in England. However, this figure does not include editions of the work published in nine other languages, and so the total figure is likely approaching 500,000. L. Venditti from the Centro Editoriale Valtortiano, e-mail correspondence, January 3, 2017.

[76] CDF, Decree placing *Il poema di Gesù* and *Il poema dell'Uomo-Dio* on the Index, December 16, 1959, in *AAS*, 52 (1960), 60 [= CDF, Decree placing *Il poema* on the Index].

[77] E. Pisani, *Pro e contro Maria Valtorta*, 5th ed., Isola del Liri (FR), Italia: Centro Editoriale Valtortiano, 2008 [= Pisani, *Pro e contro*]. See also M. Miravalle, "Response."

Corrado Berti, professor of dogmatic and sacramental theology at the Marianum Pontifical Faculty of Theology in Rome; and Fr. Andrea Cecchin, Prior of Saint Alexis Falconieri College in Rome.[78] Pius XII had been given a typewritten copy of Valtorta's still unpublished work some months earlier, and these three priests would report that Pius XII told them at the audience: "Publish this work as it is. There is no need to give an opinion about its origin, whether it be extraordinary or not. Who reads it, will understand."[79] However, in 1949, the Holy Office summoned Fr. Berti to appear before it and forbade the publication of the work.

In 1952, ten scholars, among whom was Archbishop Alfonso Carinci, Secretary of the Sacred Congregation of Rites, petitioned Pius XII to permit the work to be published.[80] Nonetheless, there was no forthcoming papal intervention and on December 16, 1959, under John XXIII, the Holy Office placed the work on the Index.[81] The decree was published in the January 6, 1960, edition of *L'Osservatore Romano*, along with an anonymous article which asserted that the work had been placed on the Index because the publisher had violated canon 1385 (*CIC*/17) which required any writings treating of religious matters to receive the imprimatur prior to publication. The

---

[78] Notice of audience with Pius XII, in *OR*, February 27, 1948, 48. Fr. Cecchin was also professor of liturgy, patristics, and patrology at the Marianum. The process for his beatification is currently underway.

[79] M. Miravalle, "Response," no. 1. See also E. Pisani, *Pro e contro*, 63.

[80] See E. Pisani, *Pro e contro*, 65–94. Msgr. Carinci was Secretary to the Congregation of Sacred Rites from 1930–1960 and charged with discerning between authentic saints and frauds. Having visited Valtorta multiple times, he had a favorable opinion of her and her writings. See also the correspondence between Msgr. Carinci and Valtorta in Valtorta, *Lettere a Mons. Carinci*, Isola del Liri (FR), Italia: Centro Editoriale Valtortiano, 2006.

[81] CDF, Decree placing *Il poema* on the Index, 60.

article went on to criticize the work's length, literary style, and content.[82]

The Index would be abrogated just a few years later, but interest in Valtorta's writings would increase significantly in the following decades. This would lead some ecclesiastical authorities to issue letters referencing that this work had been placed on the Index and that the Index's moral value endured.

3.2 – Juridic Import of Subsequent Letters from Prelates

In the decades following the Index's abrogation, Cardinal Joseph Ratzinger and Bishop Dionigi Tettamanzi wrote letters recalling that Valtorta's work had been placed on the Index and reiterating the Index's enduring moral value. Other prelates wrote letters in support of the work. We will now briefly examine the juridic import of these documents.

3.2.1 – Letters of Cardinal Ratzinger

Since the abrogation of the Index, the CDF has never issued a notification or decree with regard to Valtorta's writings. However, on January 31, 1985, Cardinal Ratzinger wrote a private letter to Cardinal Siri on the subject.[83] A priest from Cardinal Siri's diocese had written the CDF asking the position of the Magisterium with regard to the *Poem*. Ratzinger responded by writing Siri, whom he invited to share the contents of the letter with the priest concerned. The brief letter recalled the Holy Office's decree of December 16, 1959, the anonymous article printed in *L'Osservatore Romano* in 1960, and the CDF's 1966 notification on the enduring moral value of the Index. Ratzinger then added that "the diffusion and recommendation of [a

---

[82] "Una vita di Gesù malamente romanzata," in *OR*, January 6, 1960, 4.

[83] J. Ratzinger, Letter to Cardinal Giuseppe Siri, January 31, 1985, in E. Pisani, *Pro e contro*, 208.

work such as the *Poem*] is not held to be opportune when its condemnation was not taken superficially, but after weighing its purposes, to the end of neutralizing the damages which such a publication could bring to the more unprepared faithful."[84] This statement was not made in the form of an official act of the CDF, such as a decree or notification, so it is not juridically binding.

On May 21, 1993, Bishop Raymond Boland of Birmingham, Alabama, in a letter to Terry Colafrancesco, asserted that Cardinal Ratzinger had written to him on April 17, 1993, and had "asked me to inform you about the position of the Church" regarding the *Poem*. Boland asserted that the Cardinal wished to recall the items previously published in *L'Osservatore Romano* (presumably the decree of December 16, 1959, the accompanying anonymous article, and the notification of November 15, 1966). He also asserted that the CDF had asked the Italian Bishops' Conference to request of the publisher of the *Poem* that in any future edition "it might be clearly indicated from the very first page that the 'visions' and 'dictations' referred to in it are simply the literary forms used by the author to narrate in her own way the life of Jesus. They cannot be considered supernatural in origin."[85] This letter of Ratzinger was never made public; however, even if it were, it would not have any juridic weight, since it is not an official act of the Congregation.

---

[84] "...non si ritiene opportune la diffusione e raccomandazione di un'Opera la cui condanna non fu presa alla leggera ma dopo ponderate motivazioni al fine di neutralizzare i Danni che tale pubblicazione può arrecare ai fedeli più sprovveduti." J. Ratzinger, private letter to Cardinal Giuseppe Siri, January 31, 1985, in E. Pisani, *Pro e contro*, 208.

[85] R. Boland, private letter of May 21, 1993 to T. Colafrancesco, http://www.bardstown.com/~brchrys/Chrchval.html (14 April 2017).

3.2.2 – Letter of Bishop Tettamanzi

On May 6, 1992, Bishop Dionigi Tettamanzi, General Secretary to the Italian Bishops' Conference, sent a letter to Dr. Emilio Pisani, the publisher of the *Poem*. The letter recalled the decree of December 16, 1959, and the notification of November 14, 1966, and requested that, "in any future editions of the *Poem*, it be clearly indicated from the first pages that the 'visions' and the 'dictations' referred to therein cannot be considered to be of supernatural origin, but should be considered simply as literary forms which the Author made use of in order to narrate, in her way, the life of Jesus."[86] What is the juridic import of this request? Conferences of bishops can only issue juridically binding documents when certain conditions are met. For example, a conference can only issue general decrees 1) "in cases where universal law has prescribed it or a special mandate of the Apostolic See has established it;" 2) where, at a plenary meeting of the conference, two-thirds of the bishops voted in favor of the decree, and 3) where they have been reviewed by the Holy See and are then legitimately promulgated.[87] Similarly, a conference can only issue juridically binding singular administrative acts in matters for which they are competent in law, such as the erection of a national association of the faithful (c. 312 §1, 2°) or the approval of a national shrine (cc. 1231, 1232, §1). Quite often, documents issued by a conference, even

---

[86] "…sono a chiederLe che, in un'eventuale ristampa dei volumi, si dica con chiarezza fin dalle prime pagine che le 'visioni' e i 'dettati' in essi riferiti, non possono essere ritenuti di origine soprannaturale, ma devono essere considerati semplicemente forme letterarie di cui si è servita l'Autrice per narrare, a suo modo, la vita di Gesù." D. Tettamanzi, private letter to E. Pisani, May 6, 1992, in E. Pisani, *Pro e contro*, 263.

[87] *CIC*/83, c. 455.

those documents approved by a majority of the bishops at a plenary assembly, are not juridically binding.[88]

In *Apostolos suos*, John Paul II clarified that no doctrinal declarations of the conference of bishops may constitute authentic magisterium unless they are either unanimously approved by the bishops who are members of the conference, or else are approved, at a plenary meeting of the conference, by two-thirds of the bishops and also receive the *recognitio* of the Apostolic See.[89] Documents issued by the conference of bishops that do not meet those criteria only constitute authentic teaching to the degree that they repeat prior statements of the magisterium that do constitute authentic teaching. Furthermore, "no body of the conference of bishops, outside of the plenary assembly, has the power to carry out acts of authentic magisterium. The conference of bishops cannot grant such power to its commissions or other bodies set up by it.[90]

Since conferences of bishops can only exercise authentic magisterium or issue juridically binding decrees when the above criteria are met, and since they cannot delegate such powers to commissions or other such bodies, *a fortiori*, a conference is unable to delegate such powers to any individual member of the conference. Moreover, neither the conference, nor its president, nor other officials of the conference, have jurisdiction and the ability to exercise executive authority in the territory of the conference (except in specified cases where

---

[88] See for example United States Conference of Catholic Bishops, "Preaching the Mystery of Faith: The Sunday Homily," Washington, DC, USCCB, 2012.

[89] John Paul II, Apostolic letter *motu proprio* on the theological and juridical nature of conferences of bishops *Apostolos suos*, May 21, 1998, in *AAS*, 90 (1998), art. 1, 657, art. 1, English translation in *CLD*, vol. 14, 366.

[90] *ibid.*

the law, including the conference's statutes, or the Holy See grants them this authority).

The president of a conference of bishops, or any other official of the conference, does not have jurisdiction over the faithful in the territory of the conference. The officials of a conference of bishops are not like a smaller version of the Holy See with regard to the territory of the conference. Rather, the conference ordinarily facilitates consultation and collaboration among the bishops, and normally the "competence of each diocesan bishop remains intact."[91]

Consequently, Bishop Tettamanzi, as the secretary of the Italian Conference of Bishops, has no jurisdiction over Pisani, the editor of the *Poem*. Hence, Bishop Tettamanzi's request that future editions of the *Poem* indicate that the work may not be considered to be of supernatural origin has no juridic weight, and Pisani has no obligation to carry it out. Hence, Pisani is not bound to adhere to the opinion expressed by Tettamanzi on the question of the supernatural origin of the *Poem*.[92]

3.2.3 – Imprimatur Granted

On March 17, 1993, Bishop Soosa Pakiam of Trivandrum granted an imprimatur to the Malayalam translation of the *Poem*. This means that this local ordinary had judged, presumably on the basis of a censor's report, that the work contains nothing contrary to the Church's teaching on faith and morals as it is proposed by the ecclesiastical magisterium (c. 830, §2).[93]

---

[91] *CIC*/83, c. 455. See also c. 824.

[92] *A fortiori* no other member of the faithful is bound to adhere to the position proposed by Tettamanzi regarding the question of the supernatural origin of the *Poem*.

[93] See John M. Huels, *The Teaching Office of the Catholic Church: A Commentary*

A number of other bishops have written letters endorsing the *Poem*.[94] For example, Bishop Mar Joseph Kindukulam writes, "There is nothing contrary to faith and morals in this work."[95] Similarly, Bishop Roman Danylak issued an endorsement of the *Poem*.[96] All these letters have no juridic weight, since the bishops in question have no jurisdiction over the publisher and are incapable of granting an imprimatur to the work.

3.3 – Juridic Import of Testimony of Persons Later Canonized or Beatified

Recent acts of the Church in the context of the canonization process touch upon the question of the enduring juridic and moral value of the Index with regard to the *Poem*. In the Apostolic Constitution *Divinus perfectionis magister*, the Church expounds the reasons for proposing some of the faithful who were "outstanding in the practice of Christian virtues" for the "pious devotion of, and imitation by, the faithful."[97] Proposing someone for the pious devotion of the faithful means proposing him or her as a heavenly intercessor. Three significant steps occur in the later stages of the process of canonization: the promulgation of a decree on the heroic virtues of the Servant

---

on *Book III of the Code of Canon Law*, Ottawa: Faculty of Canon Law, Saint Paul University, 2017, 220–222.

[94] Photocopies of supportive letters from seven bishops in India can be seen at http://www.maria-valtorta.net/document_library.html (December 30, 2016).

[95] M. Kindukulam, letter endorsing *The Poem of the Man-God*, March 25, 1992, at ibid.

[96] A photocopy of the official letter of endorsement of the English translation of *The Poem of the Man-God* by Bishop Roman Danylak, S.T.L., J.U.D., is available here: http://www.bardstown.com/~brchrys/Bishop-Danylak-Valtorta-Endorsement.pdf

[97] John Paul II, Apostolic Constitution on the Revised Procedure in Causes of Saints *Divinus perfectionis magister*, January 25, 1983, in *AAS*, 75, I (1983), 349–355, English translation in W. Woestman, *Canonization: Theology, History, Process*, 2nd ed., Ottawa: Faculty of Canon Law, Saint Paul University, 2014, 214.

of God, the act of beatification, and the act of canonization. As Robert Sarno of the Congregation for the Causes of Saints asserts, "only beatification gives the confirmation of the intercessory power of the Servant of God."[98] Once a Servant of God has been beatified, the faithful can have full confidence in the Blessed's intercessory power and imitability.

With regard to imitability, the Church proclaims that "when we consider the life of those who have faithfully followed Christ [...] we are most safely taught the path by which [...] we can arrive at that perfect union with Christ, which is holiness."[99] This does not mean that the individual was infallible but that the Church invites the faithful to have particular confidence and trust in imitating the lives of those who have been declared blessed or canonized, assuring us that we are "most safely" taught the path by which we can arrive at holiness when we imitate them. Sarno specifies that the Church gives us the assurance that those declared blessed or who are canonized led a "totally heroically virtuous life," meaning that they practiced the four cardinal virtues and the three theological virtues to a heroic degree. The Congregation looks closely at the last five to ten years of the individual's life to "verify the reaching of a heroic practice of all the Christian virtues."[100]

Within the past five years, the Church has carried out two beatifications and a canonization with particular relevance to the current value of the Index with regard to the *Poem*. These cases will be briefly examined below to evaluate the relevance of these juridic acts in determining the current juridic and moral value of the Index with regard to the *Poem*.

---

[98] R. Sarno, e-mail reply, August 16, 2016.
[99] John Paul II, *Divinus perfectionis magister*, in Woestman, *Canonization*, 215.
[100] R. Sarno, e-mail reply, August 16, 2016.

3.3.1 – Saint Teresa of Calcutta

On September 4, 2016, Mother Teresa of Calcutta was canonized. Father Leo Maasburg,[101] who, as her confessor, traveled and worked closely with her for years, testifies as follows.

"At times, over the course of several years, I observed Mother Teresa traveling with three books: the Bible, her breviary, and a third book. When I asked her about the third book she replied that it was the *Poem of the Man-God* by Maria Valtorta. When I further asked about its contents, Mother Teresa replied, 'Read it.' The book was one of the five English volumes of 'The Poem of the Man-God.'"[102]

From the Church's act of canonizing Mother Teresa, we know that in imitating her we are "most safely taught the path" by which we can arrive at holiness, since she possessed the virtues to a heroic degree. This does not mean that she was infallible, but it does mean that her example is a relevant one when discerning the enduring moral value of the Index with regard to the *Poem*, particularly when considered in conjunction with the following examples.

3.3.2 – Blessed María Inés Teresa Arias

On April 21, 2012, María Inés Teresa Arias (1904–1981) was beatified. Foundress of the Poor Clare Missionary Sisters of the Blessed Sacrament, she wrote in 1978, "I am very attached to the reading of the work *The Poem of the Man-God*. Truly it has become one of the most beautiful sources of spiritual

---

[101] Leo Maasburg is the author of *Mother Teresa of Calcutta: A Personal Portrait*, San Francisco: Ignatius Press, 2015.

[102] L. Maasburg, affidavit, April 25, 2016, in Anthony Pillari, The Current Juridic and Moral Value of the Index of Forbidden Books, JCL thesis, Ottawa: Saint Paul University, 2017, 45.

reading."[103] In addition to using the work for her own spiritual reading, Arias promoted it to others. As Sister Urlanga testified, "our Reverend Mother liked [the *Poem*] very much and asked me to order the series of four volumes in Spanish and Italian for the thirty-five houses that she had founded up until then and that were scattered all over the world. She also gave them as gifts to Bishops, Priests, and other persons."[104] These actions were taken during the last five to ten years of Arias' life,[105] the period of a blessed's life that the Congregation for Saints scrutinizes carefully to ensure that the individual practiced heroic virtue.

3.3.3 – Blessed Gabriel Allegra

On September 12, 2012, Gabriel Allegra (1907–1976) was beatified. The only twentieth century Scriptural exegete to be beatified, he discovered Valtorta's writings in 1965 and studied them intensely. After several years of study and prayer, he wrote:

"After the Gospels, I do not know another life of Jesus that can compare to the *Poem*, as I do not know any other lives of St. Peter and St. John which make the characters of these two Apostles so alive.... In treating the mystery of Mary's

---

[103] "Io sono molto affezionata alla lettura dell'opera 'Il Poema dell'Uomo Dio.' Veramente è diventata una delle fonti di lettura spiritual più bella." M. I. T. Arias, letter expressing gratitude for the writings of Valtorta, May 22, 1978, in *ibid.*, 46.

[104] "...yo por encargo de N. Rev. Madre hice todos los pedidos para surtir a las 35 casas esparcidas por el mundo que hasta entonces habia fundado Nuestra Madre porque a ella le gustaba mucho y aparte regaló a Obispos, Sacerdotes y personas la serie de los 4 tomos en español e italiano." M.G. Uranga L., private letter, July 19, 2001, in A. Pillari, The Current Juridic and Moral Value of the Index of Forbidden Books, 47.

[105] The 1978 letter was written just three years before her death. Since the first Spanish volume did not appear until 1976, Arias' actions to obtain the work for the 35 houses she had founded and others must have taken place during the last five years of her life.

Compassion, it seems to me that Valtorta, through her breadth, profundity and psychological probing of the Heart of the Virgin, surpasses even St. Bonaventure and St. Bernard. Could she have done this without having supernaturally seen and heard?"[106]

Much impressed with the *Poem*, he urged others to read it, and he continued to study it during the last ten years of his life. He held, while respecting an eventual judgment of the Church, that the work came from the Spirit of Christ, and that "It is a work that makes one grow in the knowledge of the Lord Jesus and of His Holy Mother."[107] Such assertions are significant because they were made by one whom the Church assures us not only had to an heroic degree the virtues of prudence and faith, but who also had as his life's work the study of Sacred Scripture, who was an expert in this domain, and who analyzed the *Poem* at the peak of his scholarly knowledge.[108] By proclaiming through the beatification that, when we imitate him, we "most safely" follow the path that leads to holiness, the Church is indicating that we can safely follow his prudential judgment.

Two centuries earlier, in 1816, the Church beatified another scholar, Alphonsus Liguori. A few years after his beatification but before his canonization, and well before he was proclaimed a Doctor of the Church, the Sacred Penitentiary clarified that "one could safely follow the teaching of St. Alphonsus, without

---

[106] "Dopo i Vangeli, io non conosco un'altra vita di Gesù che si possa paragonare al Poema, come non conosco altre vite di San Pietro o San Giovanni che rendano così vivi i caratteri dei due Santi Apostoli.... Nel trattare il mistero della Compassione di Maria, pare a me che la Valtorta, per ampiezza, profondità e scandaglio psicologico del Cuore della Vergine, superi perfino San Bonaventura e San Bernardino. Poteva farlo senza aver soprannaturalmente visto e sentito?" in E. Pisani, *Pro e contro*, 129–130.

[107] *ibid.*, 143. See also *ibid.*, 121.

[108] Allegra would continue to work actively as a scholar up until the time of his death in 1976. His analysis of the *Poem* began in 1965, when he could approach the text with the benefit of forty years' experience as a Scriptural exegete.

even seeking other opinions,"¹⁰⁹ though this did not mean that Alphonsus was infallible nor that other opinions were false. While that judgment was a singular one concerning St. Alphonsus, it sheds light on how the Church's assertion, "when we consider the life of those who have faithfully followed Christ […] we are most safely taught the path by which […] we can arrive at that perfect union with Christ, which is holiness," can be received with regard to a beatified scholar.

3.4 – Current Juridic and Moral Value of the Index for the *Poem*

What, then, is the current juridic and moral value of the Index for the *Poem of the Man-God*? The Index no longer has the force of ecclesiastical law. Therefore, when one chooses to read, publish, or promote the *Poem*, there is no violation of ecclesiastical law. The various letters issued by prelates in the decades following the abrogation of the Index on the subject of the *Poem* are not juridically binding, and a Catholic is permitted to think and act in ways different from the opinions expressed in them. For example, a Catholic who believes the *Poem* to be of supernatural origin or promotes it as such is not being disobedient to Bishop Tettamanzi's letter, for the letter has no juridic weight.¹¹⁰

With regard to its current moral value, the "Index remains morally binding, in light of the demands of natural law, insofar

---

[109] A. Cummings, *The Servant and the Ladder*, Leominster, England: Gracewing, 2014, 131.

[110] In fact, the editor of the *Poem*, Emilio Pisani, has chosen to publish Tettamanzi's request at the beginning of the work, but he is not bound to do so. Regarding the degree of faith which is juridically permissible with regard to private revelations such as the *Poem* purports to be, see M. Miravalle, *Private Revelation: Discerning with the Church*, Goleta, CA: Queenship Publishing, 2007, 32–38, which presents key points of Benedict XIV's classic treatise *Heroic Virtue*.

as it admonishes the conscience of Christians to be on guard for those writings that can endanger faith and morals."[111] Hence, any Catholic considering reading a book on the Index, whether it be John Stuart Mill's *Principles of Political Economy* or the *Poem of the Man-God*, must judge whether or not the work would be nourishing for his soul or whether it would on the contrary present a proximate spiritual danger to his soul.

Catholics are free to disagree with the opinions of prelates such as Ratzinger or Tettamanzi who expressed critical opinions with regard to the *Poem*; or to disagree with prelates such as Kindukulam or Danylak who expressed favorable opinions with regard to the *Poem*.[112] The appointment of an individual to the office of prefect of the CDF, or to any other office in the Church, is not an endorsement of that individual's personal judgments and opinions. The appointment of an individual to an office does entail an obligation of obedience to their legitimate decisions, when such are given in a juridically binding form.

An appointment to an ecclesiastical office is not comparable to the trust that the Church invites the faithful to have in the opinions and advice of those who have been beatified or canonized. The Church proposes for imitation the personal lives, including the part of their lives that involved giving opinions or advice, of those beatified or canonized as a "most sure" path. For, among the virtues practiced heroically by these

---

[111] CDF Notification, in *CLD*, vol. 6, 814.

[112] A photocopy of the official letter of endorsement of the English translation of The Poem of the Man-God by Bishop Roman Danylak, S.T.L., J.U.D., is available here: http://www.bardstown.com/~brchrys/Bishop-Danylak-Valtorta-Endorsement.pdf A photocopy of Bishop Kundukulam's signed letter of endorsement is available here: http://www.maria-valtorta.net/images/malayalam_kundukulam.pdf

men and women is the virtue of prudence, so the faithful can have a degree of trust in their decisions. Therefore, St. Teresa of Calcutta's choice of the *Poem* as spiritual reading; Blessed Maria Inés Teresa Arias' discernment that the *Poem* had become "one of the most beautiful sources of spiritual reading,"[113] and her decision to promote the *Poem* in the convents she had founded and to promote it to other individuals; and Blessed Gabriel Allegra's evaluation that, after the Gospels, no other life of Christ can compare to the *Poem*, or his evaluation that the *Poem*'s description of Mary's compassion surpasses even the writings of St. Bernard and St. Bonaventure—these assertions merit particular consideration by the Christian faithful when discerning whether reading the *Poem* would be nourishing for their soul. The Church invites the faithful to consider the actions of these individuals with the confidence that "when we consider the life of those who have faithfully followed Christ [...] we are most safely taught the path by which [...] we can arrive at that perfect union with Christ, which is holiness."[114]

---

[113] "Io sono molto affezionata alla lettura dell'opera 'Il Poema dell'Uomo Dio.' Veramente è diventata una delle fonti di lettura spiritual più bella" (M. Arias, letter, May 22, 1978).

[114] John Paul II, *Divinus perfectionis magister*, in Woestman, *Canonization*, 215.

5

BLESSED GABRIEL'S CRITIQUE OF THE POEM

In June, 1970, in Macau, China, after five years of studying Valtorta's work, Blessed Gabriel Allegra composed the following introduction to the *Poem*. Because it provides a fairly complete introduction, it is presented here in its entirety:[115]

"*The Poem* contains, or rather is, a series of visions witnessed by the Writer [Valtorta] as if she were a contemporary of them. She therefore sees and hears whatever concerns the life of Jesus from the beginning of the Birth of Most Holy Mary, which occurred through a Heavenly grace in the old age of Anne and Joachim, up to the Resurrection and Ascension of the Lord—or rather, up to the Assumption of the Blessed Virgin into Heaven.

"The Visionary-Hearer usually begins by describing the location of the scene which she contemplates; she reports the chatter of the crowd and of the disciples; and then, according to what she sees and hears, she describes the miracles, relates the Discourses of the Lord, or the dialogues of those present with Him or with the disciples, or the dialogues among themselves. This re-evoking of the life of Jesus, its times and surroundings, and in its various aspects: physical, political, social, familial, is done without any effort. The Writer reports what she has seen or heard. Her style does not resound with the erudition notable in the most famous lives of Jesus. It is rather the report of an eye and auricular witness. If Mary of Magdala or Joanna of Chuza had been able during their life to see what Maria Valtorta sees, and had written it down, I believe that their testimony would not differ much from that of the *Poem*. Valtorta observed with such intensity the place and personages of her visions that anyone who has been in the Holy Land for studies and has

---

[115] The original Italian can be found in *Bollettino Valtortiano*, no. 6, September 1972, 21–24, 03036 Isola del Liri (FR), Italia: Edizioni Pisani / Centro Editoriale Valtortiano srl. Viale Piscicelli, 89/91. English translation by Br. Chrys Castel, OCSO.

repeatedly read the Gospels, need make no excessive effort to reconstruct the scene.

"That a novelist or a playwright of genius may create unforgettable characters is a known fact; but of the numerous novelists or playwrights who have approached the Gospel in order to use it in their creations, I do not know of one who has drawn from it such richness nor sketched with such force and so pleasingly the figures of Peter, John, Mary Magdalene, Lazarus, Judas—especially of Judas and his tragic and pitiful mother, Mary of Simon—and of so many, many others (and I omit for now Jesus and Mary), as does Valtorta, with the greatest naturalness and without the least effort.

The Discourses

"The most impressive thing, at least for me, are the Lord's Discourses. Naturally there are all those found in the Holy Gospels, but developed; as are also developed a good many themes which in the Gospel are barely sketched or hinted at. There are, moreover, many other Discourses reported of which nothing is said in the Gospel, but which the circumstances led Jesus to pronounce. These too are constructed as the former [i.e., as those found in the Gospel]. It is the same Lord who speaks, whether He adopts the style of the parable (the *Poem* contains some forty 'agrapha' [i.e., 'unwritten'] parables), or an exhortative or prophetic style, or finally, whether He employs the sapiential style in use among the rabbis of the New Testament epoch. Therefore, besides the great Discourses of the Gospels, such as the Sermon on the Mount, that of the Sending Out of the Apostles, the Eschatological Discourse, those of the last week and of the Last Supper, there are in the *Poem* many others, e.g., which explain the Decalogue, the corporal and spiritual works of mercy, or which constitute special instructions to the men or women disciples, to an individual person, or to mixed hearers of Jews and Gentiles.... Finally, there are the Discourses on the Kingdom of God or more clearly on the Church, which are held before the Passion as a colloquy by the Lord with His brother-cousin, James, on Carmel, and are then [further] developed after the Resurrection while He was speaking to the Apostles and the disciples on Tabor and on another mountain of Galilee. The theme of these latter is indicated by St. Luke with the simple phrase: ...*speaking of the Kingdom of God* (*cf.* 9:11).

"In briefly considering the matter treated in these Discourses, one finds in them all of the Christian Faith, Life and Hope. The tone and the style never belie themselves; they are always the same: lucid, strong, prophetic, at times full of majesty; at others, overflowing with tenderness. I will cite some examples.

"We all know the anxiety of the greatest exegetes to situate and explain according to their living context, e.g., the colloquy with Nicodemus, the Discourse on the Bread of Life, the theological-polemical Discourses pronounced at Jerusalem: how many efforts made and how varied! In the *Poem*, however, their connection is spontaneous and natural, as if flowing logically from the circumstances.

The Events

"What is said of the Discourses is also valid for the miracles. In the *Poem* there are so many of them, which the Gospel subsumes under the phrase: "and He cured and healed all." There are also some events which neither exegetes, nor novelists, nor the apocryphal writers have thought of. For example, the evangelization of Judea hinted at by St. John (*Jn* 1–4) at the beginning of the ministry of Jesus; the merciful apostolate of the Lord in favor of the Samaritans, of the poor, of the peasant-farmers of Doras and Giocana, of the inhabitants of the district of Ophel; the continuous journeys of the tireless Master through the territory of all the twelve ancient tribes; and the conspiracy plotted, by some in good faith, by most in bad faith, to proclaim Him king and thus to destroy Him more easily by Roman hands—a plot which John (*Ch. 6*) soberly hints at.

"And how could one forget the heroic fidelity of the twelve Bethlehem shepherds and the double imprisonment of John the Baptist? and those converted by the convert, Zaccheus, and those persons whom Jesus saved even materially, like Syntyche, Aurea Galla, Benjamin of Aenon? Or again, the last prophetic voices of the chosen People: Sabea of Bethlechi, the healed Samaritan leper, and Saul of Keriot? Or how could one forget the relationship of Jesus with Gamaliel, with some of the members of the Sanhedrin, with a group of pagan women who gravitated around Claudia Procula, the wife of Pontius Pilate? Or the story and figure of Mary Magdalene and that of the little boy, Marjiam? Or of the individual Apostles, each of whose character is indelibly impressed in the heart of the attentive reader: especially the characters of Peter, John, and Judas and his pious and unfortunate mother?

The Palestinian World

"And how much do we not learn about the political, religious, economic, social and familial situation of Palestine in the first age of our era, even from the discourses of the most humble—rather, especially from these—which the seeing and hearing Writer, Valtorta, reports! One might say that in this Work the Palestinian world of the time of Jesus comes back to life before our eyes; and the best and worst elements of the characters of the chosen People—a people of extremes and enslaved by every mediocrity—leap alive before our eyes.

Private Revelation

"*The Poem* is presented to us as the completion of the four Gospels and a long explanation of them; Valtorta, the Writer, is the illustrator of the Gospel scenes. This explanation and completion is justified in part by the words of St. John: 'Many other prodigies Jesus did before His disciples, which are not written in the present book...' (*Jn 20:30*); and: 'Many other things Jesus did which, if they had to be written one by one, I think that the whole world could not contain the books to be written' (*Jn 21:25*). It is a completion and explanation which is justified, I repeat, only in part or in principle, since from the historical-theological point of view, Revelation was closed with the Apostles and all that is added to the revealed Deposit, even if it does not contradict it but happily completes it, could at most be the fruit of a particular individual charism which obliges to faith the one who receives it, as also those who believe it to be a question of a true charism or charisma—which in our case would be the charism of revelation, of vision, or of discourses of wisdom and discourses of knowledge (*1 Cor 12:8; 2 Cor 12:1...*).

"In summary, the Church has no need of this Work to unfold Her salvific mission until the Second Coming of the Lord, as She had no need of the Apparitions of the Madonna at La Salette, at Lourdes, at Fatima.... But the Church can tacitly or publicly recognize that certain private revelations can be useful for the knowledge and practice of the Gospel and for understanding its mysteries, and hence, She can approve them in a negative form, that is, by declaring that the revelations are not contrary in word to the Faith. Or She can officially ignore them, leaving Her children full liberty to form their own judgment.

"In this negative form the revelations of St. Bridget, of St. Matilda, St. Gertrude, Venerable Mary of Agreda, St. John Bosco and many other saints have been approved."

Comparison with Other Works

"Whoever starts out to read [the *Poem*] with an honest mind and with commitment can well see for himself the immense distance that exists between the *Poem* and the *New Testament Apocrypha*, especially the *Infancy Apocrypha* and the *Assumption Apocrypha*. And he can also notice what distance there is between this Work and that of Venerable Catherine Emmerich, Mary of Agreda, etc. In the writings of these latter two visionaries, it is impossible not to sense the influence of third persons, an influence which it seems to me must on the contrary be absolutely excluded from our *Poem*. To be convinced of this it suffices to make a comparison between the vast and sure doctrine—theological, biblical, geographical, historical, topographical—which crowds every page of the *Poem*, and the same material in the [other visionary] works mentioned above. I am not going to speak of literary works, because there are none which cover the life of Jesus beginning from the Birth to the Assumption of the Madonna, or at least none known to me. But even if we limit ourselves to the basic plots of the most celebrated ones, such as: *Ben Hur, The Robe, The Great Fisherman, The Silver Chalice, The Spear*..., these could not quite bear comparison with the natural, spontaneous plot welling up from the context of events and characters of so many persons—a veritable crowd!– which forms the mighty framework of the *Poem*.

"I repeat: it is a world brought back to life, and the Writer rules it as if she possessed the genius of a Shakespeare or a Manzoni. But with the works of these two great men, how many studies, how many vigils, how many meditations are required! Maria Valtorta, on the contrary, even though possessing a brilliant intelligence, a tenacious and ready memory, did not even finish her secondary education; she was for years and years afflicted with various maladies and confined to her bed, had few books—all of which stood on two shelves of her bookcase—did not read any of the great commentaries on the Bible—which could have justified or explained her surprising scriptural culture—but just used the popular version of the Bible of Fr. Tintori, O.F.M. And yet she wrote the ten volumes of the *Poem* from 1943 to 1947, in four years!"[116]

Striking Details

"We all know how much research scholars have done, especially Hebrew scholars, in designing various maps of the political geography of Palestine from the time of the Maccabees up to the insurrection of Bar Kohkba. For more than twenty years they have had to consult a pile of documents: the Talmud, Flavius Josephus, Inscriptions, Folklore, ancient itineraries.... And yet, the identification of a good many localities still remains uncertain. In the *Poem* though—whatever could be the judgment given about its origin—there is no uncertainty. At least in 4/5ths of the cases, recent studies confirm the identifications supposed in [the *Poem*]; and the number would grow, I think, if some specialist would be willing to study this question deeply. Valtorta, for example, sees the forking of roads, landmarks which indicate directions, various cultivations according to the

---

[116] Maria started attending boarding school in March 1909. However, her mother demanded that she leave schooling in February 1913, which she was obliged to do. In spring 1913, the Valtorta family moved to Florence because her father retired for health reasons and Valtorta was not given the opportunity to continue a formal education.

differing quality of the terrain, so many Roman bridges thrown across various rivers or streams, and springs that are lively in certain seasons and dried up in others. She notes the difference in pronunciation between the various inhabitants of diverse regions of Palestine, and a mass of other things which perplex the reader, or at least make him thoughtful.

"There are a series of visions in which the mystery of the Birth of Jesus, His Agony, His Passion, and His Resurrection are described with Heavenly words and images with an angelic eloquence; while on the other hand, so much light is thrown on the mystery of Judas, on the attempt to proclaim Jesus king, on His two brother-cousins who do not [initially] believe in Him, on the impression awakened in the Gentiles about Him, on His love of the lepers, the poor, the aged, children, the Samaritans, and especially on His love, so pleasingly ardent and delicate, for His Immaculate Mother.

"And not only from the human point of view, but especially from a theological one, who can remain indifferent reading the two chapters on the desolation of His most holy Mother after the tragedy of Calvary, which reveal to us how the Co-redemptrix had been tempted by Satan, and how Her Redeemer-Son had been tempted? The sublime theology of these two chapters may be compared to that of so many of the laments of the Sorrowful Mother."

Historical-Doctrinal Harmony

"Exegetes today, even Catholics, take the strangest and most daring liberties over the historicity of the Gospel's Infancy accounts and the narratives of the Resurrection, as if with Form Criticism ['Formgeschichte'] and Redaction Criticism ['Redaktionsgeschichte Methode'] one finds the panacea for all difficulties—difficulties which were not unknown to the

Fathers of the Church. Truly, to speak only of some recent exegetes: e.g., Fouard, Sepp, Fillion, Lagrange, Ricciotti..., on these difficult points they spoke their balanced and luminous words. But today there are other masters whom even our own follow with such confidence.... Well then, to come back to us: I invite the readers of the *Poem* to read the pages consecrated to the Resurrection and to the reconstruction of the events of the day of the Pasch, and they will ascertain how all is harmoniously bound together there—just as so many exegetes who follow the critical-historical-theological method have tried to do, but without fully succeeding. Such pages [in the *Poem*] do not disturb, but rather gladden the heart of the faithful and strengthen their faith!

Language

"But there is another surprise: this woman of the 20th century who, though confined to a bed of pain, became the fortunate contemporary and follower of Christ, heard the Apostles and Jesus talk in Italian, but in an Aramaicized Italian—except for certain moments carefully noted by her: when, that is, the Apostles and Jesus prayed in Hebrew or in Aramaic. Moreover, the Lord, the Madonna, the Apostles, even when treating of subjects dealt with in the New Testament, adopt the theological language of today, that is, the language initiated by the first great theologian, St. Paul, and enriched throughout so many centuries of reflection and meditation, and which has thus become precise, clear, and irreplaceable.

"There is in the *Poem*, therefore, a transposition, a translation of the Good News announced by Jesus into the tongue of His Church of today, a transposition willed by Him, since the Visionary was deprived of any technical theological formation. And this is, I think, in order to make us understand that the Gospel message announced today by His Church of today, and with today's language, is substantially identical with His Own preaching of twenty centuries ago."

The Valtorta Phenomenon

"A book of great bulk, composed in exceptional circumstances and in a relatively very short time: here is one aspect of the Valtorta phenomenon.

"The Writer confesses repeatedly that she is only a 'mouthpiece,' a 'phonograph,' one who writes what she sees and hears, while remaining 'crucified on a bed.' Hence, according to her, the *Poem* is not her own, it does not belong to her, it was revealed, shown to her. She does nothing else but describe what she has seen, report what she has heard, while also participating in the visions with all her heart of a woman and a devoted Christian. From this intimate participation of hers is born the antipathy she feels for Judas and, on the contrary, the intense affection she feels for John, for the Magdalene, for Syntyche…, and I do not even speak of the Lord Jesus and of the most holy Madonna towards whom at times she pours out her heart and her love with words of passionate lyricism worthy of the greatest mystics of the Church.

"In the Dialogues and Discourses which form the structure of the Work there is, in addition to an inimitable spontaneity (the Dialogues), something of the ancient and at times the hieratic (the Discourses). In sum, one hears a very good translation of an Aramaic or Hebraic manner of speaking, in a vigorous, multiform, robust Italian. It is again to be noted that in the structure of these Discourses, Jesus either moves in the wake of the great Prophets, or adapts Himself to the method of the great rabbis who explain the Old Testament by applying it to contemporary circumstances. Let us recall the Pesher

['Interpretation'] of *Habakkuk* found in Qumran and compare it (passing over the word itself) with the 'pesher' which Jesus gives us of it.

"We may also compare other explanations which the Lord gave for other passages of the Old Testament and for which we possess, in whole or in part, the commentaries of the rabbis of the 3rd or 4th Century B.C., but which obviously follow a traditional style of composition much more ancient and probably also contemporaneous with Jesus. Besides an external similarity of form, we will perceive such superiority of depth, of substance, that we will finally understand fully why the crowd said: 'No one has spoken as this Man.'"[117]

A Gift of the Lord

"I hold that the Work [of Valtorta] demands a supernatural origin. I think that it is the product of one or more charisma and that it should be studied in the light of the doctrine of charisma, while also making use of the contributions of recent studies of psychology and related sciences which certainly could not have been known by old theologians like Torquemada, Lanspergius, Scaramelli, etc.

"It is the property of charisma that they are bestowed by the Spirit of Jesus for the good of the Church, for the upbuilding of the Body of Christ; and I do not see how it can be reasonably denied that the *Poem* upbuilds and delights the children of the Church. Undoubtedly, charity is the most excellent way (*1 Cor 13:1*). It is also well known that some charisma which abounded in the primitive Church had become rarer later

---

[117] Extract taken from Blessed Gabriel Allegra's critique of Maria Valtorta's work written in June 1970 during a hospital stay in Macao. The original Italian can be found in E. Pisani, *Pro e contro Maria Valtorta* (6th Edition), Isola del Liri (FR), Italia: Centro Editoriale Valtortiano, 2017, 139–148, ISBN-13: 9788879872959.

on. But it is equally certain that they have never been wholly extinct. The Church through the centuries must test if they derive from the Spirit of Jesus or are a disguise of the spirit of darkness masquerading as an angel of light: *try the spirits, if they are of God! (1 Jn 4:1)*

"Now, without anticipating the judgment of the Church which to this moment I accept with absolute submission, I allow myself to affirm that since the principal criterion for the discernment of spirits is the Word of the Lord: *from their fruits you will know them…*, (*Mt 3:20*), and with the good fruits which the *Poem* is producing in an ever growing number of readers, I think that it comes from the Spirit of Jesus."

Further Thoughts

"That a novelist or a playwright of genius may create unforgettable characters is a known fact; but of the numerous novelists or playwrights who have approached the Gospel in order to use it in their creations, I do not know of one who has drawn from it such richness and sketched with such force and so pleasingly the figures of Peter, of John, Mary Magdalene, Lazarus, Judas—especially of Judas and his tragic and pitiful mother, Mary of Simon—and of so many, many others (and I omit for now Jesus and Mary), as does Valtorta with the greatest naturalness and without the least effort.

"[…] And how much do we not learn about the political, religious, economic, social and familial situation of Palestine in the first age of our era, even from the discourses of the most humble—rather, especially from these—which the seeing and hearing Writer, Valtorta, reports! One might say that in this Work the Palestinian world of the time of Jesus comes back to life before our eyes; and the best and worst elements of the characters of the chosen People—a people of extremes and enslaved by every mediocrity—leap alive before us.

"[...] There are a series of visions in which the mystery of the Birth of Jesus, His Agony, His Passion, and His Resurrection are described with Heavenly words and images, with an angelic eloquence; [...]

"[...] We may also compare other explanations which the Lord gave for other passages of the Old Testament and for which we possess, in whole or in part, the commentaries of the rabbis of the 3rd or 4th Century B.C., but which obviously follow a traditional style of composition much more ancient and probably also contemporaneous with Jesus. Besides an external similarity of form, we will perceive such superiority of depth, of substance, that we will finally understand fully why the crowd said: 'No one has spoken as this Man.'

"*The Poem of the Man-God* impresses me always more from the literary, exegetical, and theological point of view. As to the literary, there is no need to have recourse to preternatural gifts; the extraordinary intelligence and very acute sensitivity of Valtorta is enough to explain this Work. However, even on this point one need not forget that the Writer did not follow the chronological sequence of the life of Jesus, but that of the visions which Jesus showed her.

"And what makes me marvel the more is that Valtorta never falls into theological error; on the contrary, she renders the mysteries revealed more easy for the reader, transposing them into a popular and modern language.

"[...] Whoever reads this Work after the articles and monographs of so many modern followers of *Formgeschicte* [*Form Criticism*] and *Redaktionsgeschichte* [*Redaction Criticism*], breathes at last the atmosphere of the Gospel, and almost becomes (he may also be one of the number—but always the more fortunate—of bultmannian exegetes), he almost becomes, I say, one of the crowd which follows the Master.

"Gifts of nature and mystical gifts harmoniously joined together, explain this masterpiece of Italian religious literature, and perhaps I should say this masterpiece of literature of the Christian world.

"[...] After twenty centuries, Jesus repeats and explains His Gospel by availing Himself of all the theological terminology of His Church, so as to tell us that Her teaching is already found implicitly in His Gospel—M. Pouget would have said: equivalently—and that this teaching is none other than the authoritative and infallible explanation which She gives and She alone can give, because She is guided and illumined by the Holy Spirit.

"As to what concerns these truths, e.g., the Most Holy Eucharist, the dignity and mission of the Blessed Virgin Mary, Jesus already spoke during His life more clearly than the Church has done for centuries, so that the dogmatic progress for these and other truths is a return to the fullness of their Source.

"[...] As to the Mariology of this Work, I know of no other books which possess a Mariology so fascinating and convincing, so firm and so simple, so modern and at the same time so ancient, even while being open to its future advances. On this point the *Poem* even, or rather above all, enriches our knowledge of the Madonna and irresistibly also our poor love, our languid devotion for Her. In treating the mystery of the Compassion of Mary, it seems to me that Valtorta, by her breadth, depth, and psychological sounding of the Heart of the Virgin, surpasses even St. Bonaventure and St. Bernardine.

Could she do so without having supernaturally seen and heard?"[118]

"The great Discourses of Jesus in the *Poem of the Man-God* are framed in the ambient and circumstances which show them to us as being more spontaneous and more natural.

"The Discourses at 'Clear Water' are like the true, authentic explanation of the Decalogue; the Discourse on the Mountain is the *magna carta* of the Kingdom of Heaven. The parables [are] scattered throughout the book and always anchored to some circumstance which has given them birth and helps to understand them in depth; the great Discourses at Jerusalem, and the continuous instructions given to the Apostles, to the men and women Disciples, make of the *Poem* a coffer of Heavenly treasures.

"Noteworthy is the manner in which Jesus explains the Old Testament, applying it always to the present, to the messianic era already in progress and which is being accomplished.

"Also the discourses of the Apostles, especially those of Peter and John, are as an echo of the thought of Jesus.... I do not believe it is wise or just to remain indifferent before such treasures."[119]

"To sum up, dear Fr. Margiotti, I believe that you are an instrument of the Lord to make this soul known and its message—oh! a message so ample: ample as the Gospel!"[120]

---

[118] These passages were written by Blessed Gabriel in the late 1960s. The original Italian can be found in *Bollettino Valtortiano*, no. 29, January–June 1984, 114–116, 03036 Isola del Liri (FR), Italia: Edizioni Pisani / Centro Editoriale Valtortiano srl. Viale Piscicelli, 89/91. English translation by Br. Chrys Castel, OCSO.

[119] Letter, January 9, 1970. The original Italian can be found in *Bollettino Valtortiano*, no. 30, July–December 1984, 118, 03036 Isola del Liri (FR), Italia: Edizioni Pisani / Centro Editoriale Valtortiano srl. Viale Piscicelli, 89/91. English translation by Br. Chrys Castel, OCSO.

[120] Letter to Fr. Fortunato Margiotti in Rome, May 24, 1969. The original Italian can

"The language, more than being dignified, is fascinating; and when the Madonna is spoken of, there is a sweetness and a true Heavenly enchantment."[121]

"...I would like to write to you, as you desire, so many things on O.L. [= Our Lord] seen by one who lives in your land, but time is lacking to me; either retreats or confessions seriously bind me.... But I assure you that the *Poem of the Man-God* immensely surpasses any descriptions—I do not say of mine, because I do not know how to write—but of any other writer.

"I rejoice so much in perceiving that this Work is loved by the Poor Lady of Caltanissetta, and especially by my dearly beloved sister, Sr. Leonie. Pray to the Madonna that there be success in translating it into English, Russian and Chinese. The Spanish version is already finished.... It is a Work that makes one grow in the knowledge and love of the Lord Jesus and His Holy Mother."[122]

---

be found in *Bollettino Valtortiano*, no. 31, January–June 1985, 122, 03036 Isola del Liri (FR), Italia: Edizioni Pisani / Centro Editoriale Valtortiano srl. Viale Piscicelli, 89/91. English translation by Br. Chrys Castel, OCSO.

[121] Letter to Blessed Gabriel's uncle Joachim, Vicar in San Giovanni La Punta (Catania), August 5, 1965. The original Italian can be found in *Bollettino Valtortiano*, no. 31, January–June 1985, 122, 03036 Isola del Liri (FR), Italia: Edizioni Pisani / Centro Editoriale Valtortiano srl. Viale Piscicelli, 89/91. English translation by Br. Chrys Castel, OCSO.

[122] Letter to Blessed Gabriel's cousin Leonie Morabito, Poor Clare Sister in Caltanissetta, from Jerusalem, Monday of Holy Week, 1974. The original Italian can be found in *Bollettino Valtortiano*, no. 31, January–June 1985, 122, Edizioni Pisani / Centro Editoriale Valtortiano srl. Viale Piscicelli, 89/91, 03036 Isola del Liri (FR), Italia. English translation by Br. Chrys Castel, OCSO.

Appendix I:
Discover the *Poem* for Yourself

If you wish to discover the *Poem* for yourself, and more importantly if you wish to grow closer to Jesus Himself through the reading of the *Poem*, then you are encouraged to read the *Poem* directly. In the United States, copies can be obtained from the 101Foundation (www.101foundation.com) or directly from the Centro Editoriale Valtortiano (https://mariavaltorta.com/en). Centro Editoriale Valtortiano offers e-book versions of Valtorta's work in .ePub and .Mobi formats available for instant download from anywhere in the world. If you live in Australia, you can purchase Valtorta's work from the Maria Valtorta Readers' Group (www.valtorta.org.au). If you live in a country other than the United States or Australia, you can order directly from the Centro Editoriale Valtortiano (www.mariavaltorta.com) and can view the list of worldwide distributors here: https://mariavaltortastore.com/en/distributori.

Valtorta's Other Published Works

Her other major works are *The Notebooks: 1943*, *The Notebooks: 1944*, *The Notebooks: 1945–1950*, *The Lessons on the Epistle of St. Paul to the Romans*, *The Book of Azariah*, Valtorta's *Autobiography*, and *Quadernetti*. All can be ordered in printed book format or as ebooks, in .ePub and .Mobi format, from the Centro Editoriale Valtortiano.

The Notebooks

Maria Valtorta wrote 15,000 handwritten pages in 122 notebooks from 1943 to 1951, about 9,000 pages of which constitute the *Poem of the Man-God*. Many of the remaining 6,000 other pages were published under the title *The Notebooks*, composed of three volumes. These volumes consist of a series of reported messages and visions from God the Father, Jesus Christ, the Holy Spirit, the Blessed Mother, and various angels and saints.

Lessons on the Epistle of St. Paul to the Romans

This book consists of 48 reported dictations from the Holy Spirit to Valtorta that together constitute a commentary on this letter of St. Paul.

The Book of Azariah

Valtorta reports receiving dictations from her guardian angel that include commentary on the theme and readings from 58 Sunday Masses found in the traditional Roman Missal of the Catholic Church. The book contains all of these commentaries.

Valtorta's Autobiography

Written at the command of her confessor and completed less than a month before the beginning of her reported visions that constitute *The Poem of the Man-God*. Blessed Gabriel Allegra evaluated her autobiography in the following words:

"The *Autobiography* of Maria Valtorta departs from other similar works, even if written by saints. It is powerful and original to the point of making me think often of that of B. Cellini from its style: robust, lively, and spontaneous.

"It is moreover a dramatic book, because the drama stands out in the nature of things and facts: the drama is born, I would say, from the character of Valtorta's mother who, unfortunately, had little or nothing of the heart of a wife or mother. The description, so lively, of this egotistical woman weighs on the reader and makes him read with pain these pages of her daughter, of that daughter who becomes the 'voice' of Jesus and who writes *The Poem of the Man-God*. What a difference of character between mother and daughter! And what sort of heroism, and how much, in Maria. What a trial, what crosses, what martyrdom of the heart!

"The Valtorta family is completely opposite to that of St. Francis. In the latter, the father, Peter of Bernardone, does not understand his son, who instead was always understood by his mother, the gracious madonna Pica. In the Valtorta family, however, the father loves and understands his daughter, whom her mother does not understand at all and makes her always suffer.

"The heart of this woman is still more gloomy than that of the Prince father of the nun of Monza, and one is left so grieved by it in reading these pages because they have been written—naturally in obedience—always by her daughter.

"The style is vigorous and very lively, copious and so colorful that it perhaps surpasses that of *The Poem of the Man-God* itself. These are pages rich with thought and psychological soundings which help us to understand the spiritual physiognomy of the mouthpiece of Jesus: Maria Valtorta."[123]

On May 24, 1969, Blessed Allegra wrote to Fr. Margiotti:

"Dearest Fr. Margiotti,

"...And now I thank you for the *Autobiography* of Maria Valtorta, which absolutely occupies a place apart among all the autobiographies of men and women saints which I have read; like that of B. Cellini, it stands out among all other similar works of our literature.

"It is painful to read what it says of her mother, and yet it seems to me that it was this intimate, continuous, torturing

---

[123] These passages were written by Blessed Gabriel in the late 1960s. The original Italian can be found in *Bollettino Valtortiano*, no. 29, January–June 1984, 114–116, 03036 Isola del Liri (FR), Italia: Edizioni Pisani / Centro Editoriale Valtortiano srl. Viale Piscicelli, 89/91. English translation by Br. Chrys Castel, OCSO.

martyrdom which prepared Maria Valtorta for the sublime gifts of the visions and contemplations which she later received; in sum, it was this that had prepared her to be the mouthpiece of the Lord Jesus.

"The language seems to me more varied and vigorous than that of *The Poem of the Man-God*, which also is so fresh and lively. [...]"[124]

Quadernetti

Various other writings of Valtorta, written on loose sheets or sheet sets, and therefore not included in the *Notebooks*. Available only in Italian.

A Summa and Encyclopedia to Maria Valtorta's Extraordinary Work

This e-book gives an overview of Maria Valtorta and her primary work, *The Poem of the Man-God / The Gospel as Revealed to Me*. It discusses its importance and relevance, its history, its ecclesiastical status, how it compares to other similar private revelations, the arguments and evidence in favor of its supernatural inspiration, its critics and defenses, and the supplementary resources available for use with it.

This e-book can be downloaded from the Maria Valtorta Readers' Group here:

http://www.valtorta.org.au/Defence/Maria%20Valtorta%20Summa%20%26%20Encyclopedia.pdf

It can also be downloaded from Br. Chrys's website here: http://www.bardstown.com/~brchrys/Summa.pdf

---

[124] Letter to Fr. Fortunato Margiotti in Rome, May 24, 1969. The original Italian can be found in *Bollettino Valtortiano*,. no. 31, January--June 1985, 122, 03036 Isola del Liri (FR), Italia: Edizioni Pisani / Centro Editoriale Valtortiano srl. Viale Piscicelli, 89/91. English translation by Br. Chrys Castel, OCSO.

The above e-book was mentioned in a 2016 Zenit News article: http://www.valtorta.org.au/zenit-valtorta-science-and-faith-converge.html

Website Resources

The following link has a large amount of information about Maria Valtorta and the *Poem of the Man-God*: http://www.bardstown.com/~brchrys/

For resources in French, see Maria-Valtorta.org.

Maria Valtorta Readers' Group

Established in 1996, the Readers' Group is a non-profit organization, based in Melbourne, Australia. Its members include laity, priests, and religious from around the world. The Readers' Group publishes a quarterly bulletin and offers publications of Maria Valtorta's writings in books and booklets, audio CDs and other supporting materials.

Home page: http://www.valtorta.org.au/

Maria Valtorta App for iPhones, Androids, and Tablets

Features:
- Excerpts from the *Poem* for all of the Sunday Gospel readings of the liturgical year as well as some additional feast days.
- Audio recordings of the Gospel for that Sunday, followed by the corresponding passage from the *Poem*.
- 100 reported parables of Jesus from Maria Valtorta's writings.
- Additional information about Maria Valtorta and her works.

Available in English, Italian, Spanish, and French. Can be downloaded for free from: http://app.fondazionemariavaltortacev.org.

Maria Valtorta Conferences

To date, these have been held in Italy, France, and Australia. For more information see: http://www.valtorta.org.au/Maria-Valtorta-Conferences.html.

The Publisher and International Distributor of Valtorta's Writings

The publisher and international distributor of Maria Valtorta's writings is the Centro Editoriale Valtortiano in Italy: https://mariavaltorta.com/en.

If interested in making donations to promote the cause and works of Maria Valtorta, please consider donating to the Fondazione Maria Valtorta CEV (The Maria Valtorta Foundation), a non-profit organization in charge of preserving and operating the Valtorta House-Museum in Viareggio, Italy, the digitalization and preservation of her original Italian manuscripts, Valtorta translation endeavors, and other activities in the promotion of her writings. For more information see: http://fondazionemariavaltortacev.org/en.

The Virgin Mary in the Writings of Maria Valtorta by Fr. Gabriel Roschini, O.S.M.

Fr. Gabriel Roschini, O.S.M., was a world-renowned Mariologist, decorated professor and founder of the Marianum Pontifical Faculty of Theology in Rome, professor at the Lateran Pontifical University, and a Consultant to the Holy Office and the Sacred Congregation for the Causes of Saints. Fr. Roschini had personally met Maria Valtorta, but admitted that, like many others, he was initially a respectful and condescending skeptic.

However, after carefully studying her writings for himself, he underwent a radical change of heart.

Fr. Gabriel Roschini, O.S.M., wrote in the preface of his book, The *Virgin Mary in the Writings of Maria Valtorta*:

"I have been studying, teaching, preaching, and writing Mariology for half a century already. To do this, I had to read innumerable works and articles of all kinds on Mary: a real Marian library.

"However, I must candidly admit that the Mariology found in all of Maria Valtorta's writings—both published or unpublished—has been for me a real discovery. No other Marian writings, not even the sum total of everything I have read and studied, were able to give me as clear, as lively, as complete, as luminous, or as fascinating an image, both simple and sublime, of Mary, God's Masterpiece.

"It seems to me that the conventional image of the Blessed Virgin, portrayed by myself and my fellow Mariologists, is merely a paper mache Madonna compared to the living and vibrant Virgin Mary envisioned by Maria Valtorta, a Virgin Mary perfect in every way.

"...whoever wants to know the Blessed Virgin (a Virgin in perfect harmony with the Holy Scriptures, the Tradition of the Church, and the Church Magisterium) should draw from Valtorta's Mariology.

"If anyone believes my declaration is only one of those ordinary hyperbolic slogans abused by publicity, I will say this only: let them read before they judge!"[125]

---

[125] G. Roschini, *The Virgin Mary in the Writings of Maria Valtorta*, Kolbe Publications Inc, 1989, Foreword, ISBN-13: 9788879870863.

To place the quotation in context, he had published over 790 articles and miscellaneous writings, and 130 books, 66 of which were over 200 pages long—almost all on Mariology.

Dr. Mark Miravalle, S.T.D. (Doctor of Sacred Theology), wrote:

"The extensive Mariology contained in *The Poem* was also the subject of a 400-page study written by arguably the greatest Italian Mariologist of the twentieth century and Consultor of the Holy Office, Rev. Gabriel Roschini, O.S.M. In a letter of January 17, 1974, Father Roschini received the congratulations of Pope Paul VI for his work entitled, *The Virgin Mary in the Writings of Maria Valtorta*. The letter from the Secretary of State notes, 'The Holy Father thanks you wholeheartedly for this new testimony of your respectful regards and wishes you to receive from your labor the consolation of abundant spiritual benefits.' Neither the papal benediction granted by Pope Paul VI nor the papal congratulations issued through the Secretary of State would have been granted to a text based on a series of private revelations which were 'forbidden' or declared 'doctrinally erroneous' by the Congregation for the Doctrine of the Faith."[126]

You can buy Fr. Roschini's book, *The Virgin Mary in the Writings of Maria Valtorta*, at numerous online bookstores.

---

[126] M. Miravalle, *In Response to Various Questions Regarding "The Poem of the Man-God,"* April 15, 2006. http://www.valtorta.org.au/Valtorta-Miravalle.html

Resources for the *Poem*: Atlases, Indexes, Scripture-*Poem* Cross-References, Chapter Summaries, Travel Guides, Date/Timeline Guides, and More

There are numerous atlases, indexes, Scripture-*Poem* cross-references, chapter summaries, travel guides, date/timeline guides, and other resources to use with Valtorta's work. For more information about these resources, please see the relevant chapter in *A Summa and Encyclopedia to Maria Valtorta's Extraordinary Work*, which is available here: http://www.bardstown.com/~brchrys/Summa.pdf

Books Available in Other Languages

To see the catalog of books in the Italian language at the Centro Editoriale Valtortiano (the publisher and distributor of Maria Valtorta's works for all major languages), visit: https://mariavaltortastore.com/it.

The book *Pro e contro Maria Valtorta* (*For and against Maria Valtorta*), contains a large number of primary sources.

Appendix II:
Documents Regarding Testimony of St. Teresa of Calcutta and Blessed María Inés

Fr. Anthony Pillari
St. Clement Parish
528 Old St. Patrick Street
Ottawa, ON K1N 5L5
Canada

Testimony of Fr. Leo Maasburg
Regarding Blessed Mother Teresa and the Works of Maria Valtorta

I, Father Leo Maasburg, affirm the accuracy of the following from my personal travels with her:

At times, over the course of several years, I observed Mother Teresa traveling with three books: the Bible, her breviary, and a third book. When I asked her about the third book she replied that it was the *Poem of the Man-God* by Maria Valtorta. When I further asked about its contents, Mother Teresa replied "read it." The book was one of the five English volumes of "The Poem of the Man-God."

_____   25/4/16
Fr. Leo Maasburg   Date

CASA GENERALIZIA
MISSIONARIE CLARISSE

DEL SANTISSIMO
SACRAMENTO

Roma, 22 maggio 1978.

Gentilissimo Signor Pisani:

   La ringrazio molto vivamente per il prezioso omaggio fattoci da Lei: "I QUADERNI DEL 1943" e "LEZIONI SULL'EPISTOLA DI PAOLO AI ROMANI" ambe due della scrittrice María Valtorta.

   Io sono molto affezionata alla lettura dell'opera "IL POEMA DELL'UOMO DIO". Veramente è diventata una delle fonti di lettura spirituale più bella. Per questo mi auguro che gli scritti suddetti siano oltre che belli interesanti.

   Grazie di nuovo signor Pisani per il suo prezioso regalo, che ho già cominciato a leggere. Io di solito lavoro fino all'una o due del mattino e poi, prima di addormentarmi faccio la mia meditazione nella quiete della notte e mi godo i miei libri.

   Tanti cari saluti a Lei e a la signora, e sto in attesa del giorno in cui -come me lo avete promesso- posiate accetare il mio invito a pranzare da noi.

   Ossequi,

       María Inés-Teresa Arias,
       Missionaria Clarissa.
       Superiora Generale.

Sig. Emilio Pisani.
Tipografia E. Pisani.
03036 ISOLA DEL LIRI
(FROSINONE)

00187 ROMA · VIA CARDINALE GARAMPI, 17

Missionarie Clarisse del Santissimo Sacramento
Casa Generalizia

Roma, 19 de Julio del 2001.-

Estimado Sr. Emilio Pisani:

    Soy una Misionera Clarisa (hija de la Madre Ma. Inés Teresa Arias) que Usted conoció y que ella tanto estimaba.

    Cuando empezó a salir el Poema del Hombre. Dios yo por encargo de N. Rev. Madre hice todos los pedidos para surtir a las 35 casas esparcidas por el mundo que hasta entonces había fundado Nuestra Madre porque a ella le gustaba mucho y aparte regaló a Obispos, Sacerdotes y personas la serie de los 4 tomos en español e italiano.

    Ahora por lo que le escribo ésta es porque la Superiora de Irlanda me pide el tomo No. 5 en español y ya lo busqué en las mas grandes librerías de Roma (sobre todo las que venden libros en español) y no lo encontré y con gran sorpresa me enteré de que ya no lo editan y en cambio ha salido otro nuevo de la misma autora pero la Hna. quiere el 5o en español porque tiene los 4 anteriores.

    Yo quería pedirle que si por caso tiene alguno en su imprenta (tipografía) que haya quedado escondidito me lo mandara por correo a la dirección que va en el sobre y llegando a Roma le mando el importe - solo le pido me mande decir el precio.

    Si no tuviera en su casa ese tomo le pido me indique donde lo puedo conseguir. Se lo agradeceré mucho.

    Las demás casas todas tenemos la serie de los 4 primeros y algunas el No. 5o y ahora que nos enteramos que ya no editan el Poema del H. D. nos da mucha pena.

    Agradeciéndole y pidiéndole perdón por escribirle en español (no se escribir en Italiano) me despido con saludos para la Si.ra Claudia y para Ud. mi afecto de siempre.

tel: 88521625 y 88521721
FAX: 88 045 27

Maria Gpe. Uranga L.
Misionera Clarisa

About The Authors

Fr. Anthony Pillari, J.C.L, M.C.L., S.T.B., is a priest of the Diocese of Plymouth, England, where he is the Promoter of Justice and chaplain for the *usus antiquior*. He holds degrees in philosophy from the University of Notre Dame, Indiana, sacred theology from L'Institut Catholique de Toulouse, France, and canon law from the University of St. Paul and from the University of Ottawa, Canada.

Stephen Austin holds an honors degree in civil engineering from Kansas State University, is currently pursuing a Masters of Engineering in Project Management from the University of Kansas, and has been researching Maria Valtorta and her works for the past seven years. He is the author of *A Summa and Encyclopedia to Maria Valtorta's Extraordinary Work* and has spoken  at an international conference in Italy, on Australian television, and on New York Radio. The webmaster of several Valtorta websites, he continues to publish news, research, and materials on Maria Valtorta and her writings.

www.ingramcontent.com/pod-product-compliance
Lightning Source LLC
Chambersburg PA
CBHW020700300426
44112CB00007B/463